CONTENTS

Sec		*Page*
Introduction		3

CHAPTER 1—THE REASONS FOR CONCEALMENT

CHAPTER 2—THE AIR VIEW

CHAPTER 3—PRINCIPLES OF CONCEALMENT—INDIVIDUAL

CHAPTER 4—PRINCIPLES OF CONCEALMENT—UNITS AND SUB-UNITS

CHAPTER 5—ARTIFICIAL AIDS TO CONCEALMENT

CHAPTER 6—CONCEALMENT OF INFANTRY AND THEIR WEAPONS

CHAPTER 7—THE CONCEALMENT OF WHEELED VEHICLES

CHAPTER 8—CONCEALMENT OF ARMOURED FIGHTING VEHICLES

CHAPTER 9—THE CONCEALMENT OF ARTILLERY

CHAPTER 10—THE CONCEALMENT OF HEADQUARTERS, ADMINISTRATIVE AND MAINTENANCE AREAS AND COMMUNICATIONS

APPENDIXES

CONCEALMENT IN THE FIELD
1957

INTRODUCTION

The photographs in this pamphlet have been specially chosen to illustrate aspects of concealment and do not necessarily reflect current operational or training techniques in other respects. These aspects are co-ordinated in three main pointers as follows:—

1. Aim

To assist the junior leader to conceal his men and equipment.

2. Reason

Concealment gives two advantages; it achieves surprise and gives protection.

3. Method

Concealment is protection against visual observation from the ground and from the air.

To give this practical illustration, photographs taken on active service and on battle training are used.

CHAPTER 1—THE REASONS FOR CONCEALMENT

SECTION 1—Basic principles

1. Concealment is not an end in itself. It is practised to enable the Army to operate efficiently, to effect surprise and to avoid casualties.

2. The essential qualities for good concealment are:—

    (a) Power of observation. Concealment requires the study of your surroundings and the ground. You must know the picture you present to the enemy view; at close range, from a distance and from the air.

    (b) Alertness. Mistakes caused through lack of foresight are most difficult to rectify. Complacency over concealment is a frequent cause of its failure. Alertness to preserve concealment must be a habit at all times.

    (c) Adaptability. Changes of light, weather and site bring alterations that affect your concealment. Concealment measures in one place or at one time of day may prove unsuitable in another place or at another time of day.

3. Successful concealment depends on good siting. Artificial aids to concealment play but a minor role in comparison with the skilful use of all the surface features of the ground.

4. As the soldier fights on the ground, he must learn to conceal himself there in any surroundings. He has to guard against:—

    (a) Observation from the ground.

    (b) Observation from the air.

Ground observation from a fixed point

5. From this hill-top it is possible to keep the countryside under observation. Every change in the landscape is noted as it occurs.

Plate 1 (War—France)

Provence: Plain of La Crau near Toulon from an abandoned German OP

6. What could the observer see?

    (a) Movement. Movement along roads and paths, across fields and near houses. The trend of movement reveals positions and may disclose intentions. It always catches the eye.

    (b) Shape. New shapes and any alterations to existing shapes in the scene. Men, vehicles, weapons, digging, dumps and damage are all noted as they appear.

    (c) Shine. Shine from flat surfaces, shine from maps and human skin. Flashes from moving objects as they turn into the sun.
By night, any form of lights and reflection.

    (d) Shadow. New and denser shadows altering in shape as the sun moves.

    (e) Colour. The appearance of odd and contrasting colours unusual to the scene. Alterations in vegetation colouring due to damage or neglect.

All these features must be controlled to achieve concealment.

Observation on the move

7. Here is the soldier searching as he moves.

Plate 2 (War—Douet—Normandy)

He has the mind of a hunter, trying to discover before he is seen himself.

His duty compels him to keep moving so he has not much time for observation. He is alert for any clue that may disclose an enemy.

He is equally alert to find cover for himself from which he can stalk his enemy.

He must know how to find good cover readily and how to choose his way with foresight for that purpose.

Qbservation from the air

8. The enemy reconnaissance aircraft can cover the ground from many angles. The airman's camera can record anything that may catch the pilot's eye.

Plate 3. Infantry positions on farmland (Training—Germany)

Soldiers prepare a position that gives good cover from enemy ground observation. But as the sites selected disregard the ground pattern as seen from the air, they stand revealed in accurate detail for enemy observation and attack.

9. The soldier must learn how to merge himself and his equipments into the ground pattern.

Plate 4 (Training—England)

Siting comparisons

A. Our attention is attracted by the vehicles badly sited, though netted and dispersed out in the open.

B. We overlook the other vehicles well sited and netted within the shadow pattern of the hedgerows.

SECITON 2—EFFECTS OF LIGHT

Daylight

10. **Shadows move.** Many mistakes in concealment arise from this factor.

11. For example, a well netted and garnished tank is concealed beneath these trees.

This is how it appears:—

(a) In the morning.

Plate 5

(Light behind the cover. Shape tends to show against a bright background.)

(b) At noon.

Plate 6

(Light tends to show by shine and shape against the dark background of shade.)

(c) In the evening.

Plate 7

(Light shines low and tends to reveal the net and shows a contrast with the surroundings by direct illumination of the sides of the tank).

Paint

12. It is unwise to place too much faith in paint for concealment. The present policy is to discontinue the use of disruptive patterns painted on equipment and vehicles, as they are liable to fail at certain angles to the sun and against certain backgrounds.

Plate 8 (Training—Ceylon)

This carrier was painted to match the scene, but the reflection of the sun on its flat metal surfaces defeats the aim.

13. The present policy is to paint vehicles and equipment to blend with the basic colour of the land in colour and in tone.

By good siting, vehicles and equipment merge with the background.

For disruptive effects we rely on the use of cover and the natural effects of shade.

Plate 9 (War—Mandalay—Burma—1944)

At a distance the shadows of the tree trunks and branches will break up the outlines of the tank and the paint matches the ground in colour and tone. Under these combined effects a tank merges into its background.

Contrast

14. Strong contrasts break up outlines and give different depths in appearance.

Plate 10 (Training—Canada)

This Canadian sniper shows how to use colour contrasts to confuse the eye.

His white jacket, hood and gloves and white binding on his rifle blend with the snow background.

His dark clothing and weapon links up with the timber and other dark objects.

The eye fails to see the man's figure clearly as a whole

Shine

15. Shine neutralizes concealment.

Shine only appears to a viewer at certain angles to the light. This danger may not appear to those near an object, while it exists with dazzling effect to the eyes of a distant observer.

As the angle of light alters during the day so does the angle of shine. Objects that appear dull in dull weather may suddenly shine brilliantly in the sunlight. This risk is always present after rain.

Plate 11 (Training—England)

Brilliant shine, from the gun barrel of this BAT, will pierce through concealment precautions unless the object that is prone to shine is masked from the sun.

Conclusion

16. The soldier must learn to recognize the need to fit into the ground pattern over which he fights as it is observed:

> *(a)* from the ground.

> *(b)* from the air.

17. He must know the features in this pattern that will help him to conceal and also those that will hinder him.

> *(a)* He must adapt and control the shape, shine, shadow, colour and movement of his own body and equipment.

> *(b)* He must keep alert for the changes of light, weather and wear which may prejudice the effectiveness of his concealment.

> *(c)* He must know how to make proper use of the artificial aids to concealment.

CHAPTER 2—THE AIR VIEW

SECTION 3—Air observation

18. Concealment against air observation is vital. Positions may be well concealed from ground observation but remain obvious from the air.

19. There are two types of air observation against which the soldier must conceal:

    (a) Low level fighter reconnaissance.

    (b) High level photographic reconnaissance.

20. Fighter reconnaissance aircraft also carry cameras and the subsequent photographs will augment and enlarge upon what the pilot sees, in many cases showing details invisible to the naked eye.

21. Photographic reconnaissance is carried out at very high altitudes, so high that the aircraft may not be seen or even heard, and the man on the ground will have no warning that he is being observed and photographed. With modern developments in cameras and associated equipment great detail can be shown on photographs taken from these high altitudes.

It is generally more important in the strategical than tactical sense.

22. The following photographs give a good idea of what the pilot sees under various conditions and the type of photograph he will take. These photographs are developed and printed at high speed and are quickly in the hands of the photo interpreters.

Low level oblique photographs

23. The aircraft can approach from any direction. An oblique photograph will pierce some distance beneath good overhead cover.

Plate 12

Plate 13

Vertical photographs

24. These photographs give a plan view of the ground and cover a wide area.
This type of photograph can also be used to obtain stereoscopic views.

Plate 14

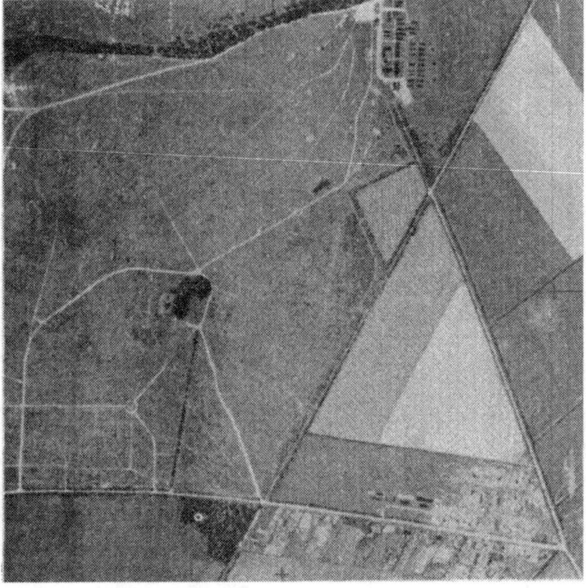

Plate 15

Light and shade from clouds

25. The contrast of the sunlit areas and the cloud formations hampers observation of the ground.

Plate 16 (Germany)

Moonlight photography

26. Even at night, roads, rivers and railways reflect light. Reflection is also apparent from roofs of buildings and military installations. The shadows cast by buildings, etc, are an aid to concealment.

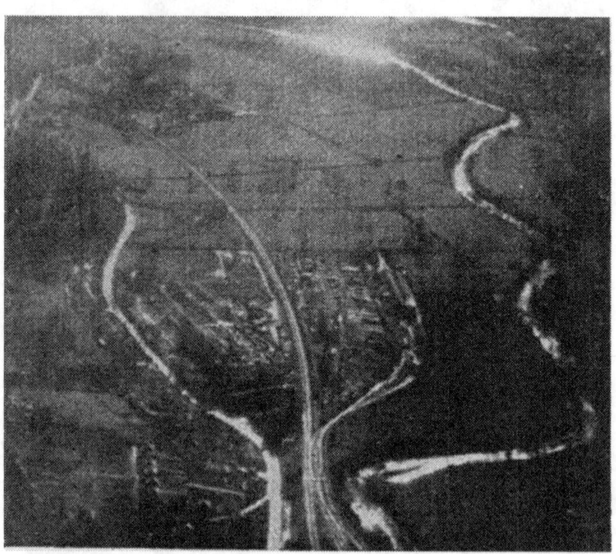

Plate 17

Infra-red photography

27. This type of photography is often used to detect camouflage.

Plate 18—Taken with an ordinary panchromatic film.

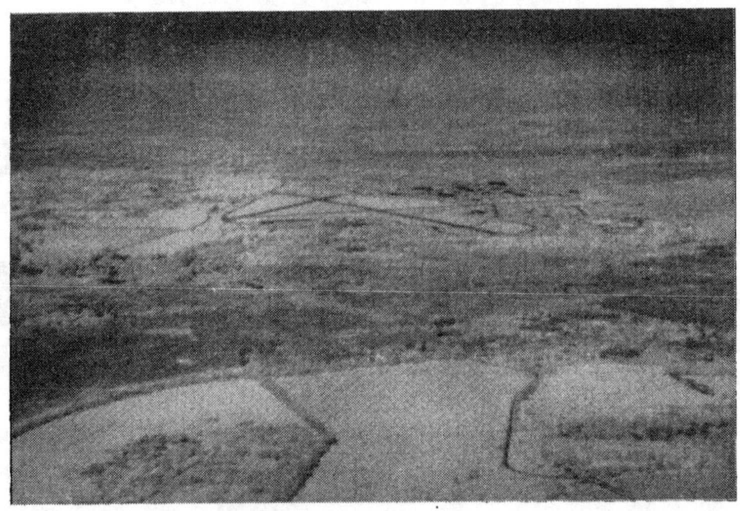

Plate 19—The same scene taken with an infra-red film.

28. Infra-red film tends to accentuate the contrast between living and dead material. Note how prominent are the airfield runways. Growing grass, crops and shrub produce a light tone whereas dead vegetation and most military material reproduces in a darker tone. Some paints and camouflage materials even of light colour reproduce as dark tones on infra-red film but detection can be avoided by using fresh vegetation as garnish. Good visual concealment using fresh natural garnish will provide good infra-red concealment.

Military signatures

29. From 4,500 feet the pattern of enemy anti-aircraft gun pits on either side of the river establish the type of weapons they contain.

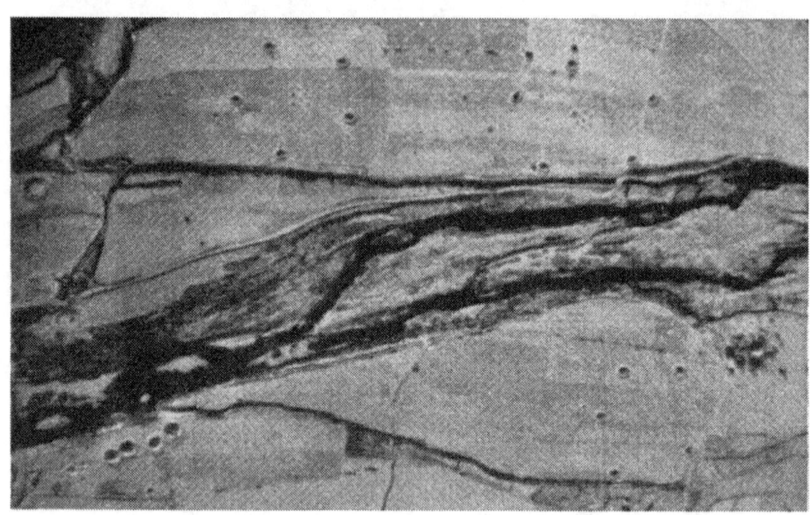

Plate 20 (War—Korea—HMS Glory)

Plate 21

These troop positions laid out in uniform pattern draw attention to the fact that guns are concealed although the weapons are not apparent.

The observer's opinion is also confirmed by the badly sited vehicles on the roadside standing in the open with no attempt at concealment

Tracks

30. Tracks of vehicles and men show up clearly to the air observer, particularly when they do not follow the ground pattern.

Trampled areas around sites also reveal clearly to the air the presence of human activities.

Tracks are more noticeable to the air than to the ground observer.

To the air view, shadows are often more readily recognizable than the shapes that cast them.

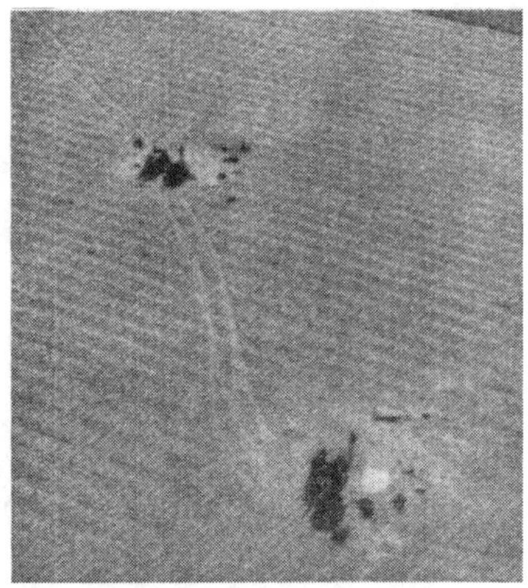

Plate 22

Litter

31. Domestic litter left in the open will attract attention.

Plate 23

Smoke

32. Smoke is most conspicuous from the air and invites closer inspection.

Plate 24

From the ground the smoke of your camp fire may appear thin as it disperses into the brightness of the sky.

Plate 25

But looking down from above, an airman may see your smoke as dense as this against the ground. Avoid fire using wood and paper and for cooking purposes use only the issue type cooker.

CHAPTER 3—PRINCIPLES OF CONCEALMENT—INDIVIDUAL

SECTION 4—Personal concealment—mental, material, physical

Attitude of mind

33. The soldier must possess the skill for concealment combined with determination in aggression like a beast of prey.

The enemy is our prey. We practice concealment as an aid to hunt and destroy him.

Plate 26 Leopard (Wajir, Kenya)

The leopard flattens himself into the ground to hide his shape and shadow. He uses the growing vegetation to break his outline. His colour matches his surroundings in contrasts and tones. He is still: no needless movement reveals his intent to attack.

Plate 27 Leopardess (Wajir, Kenya)

Moving along a line of shadow, the leopardess makes full use of every tuft of cover the ground offers. There is nothing static in her use of concealment.

Discipline

34. In action the need for care is easy to understand but it also applies to every point at which the enemy can observe a man

Plate 28 (War—Burma—1943)
An example of lack of camouflage discipline

Human shape

35. A man's body has a distinctive shape which his background may reveal. Keep within cover that breaks up your outline.

Plate 29

Mau-Mau operations: Mount Kenya

There are three men in this picture of a Kenya patrol. One is obvious but can you discover the other two?

Silhouette

36. When your background is the sky it will always reveal you from any angle. Your background, to the enemy, is not necessarily behind you.

Plate 30

No matter what aids to concealment you may use, your silhouette will betray you.

Plate 31 (War—Normandy)

This example illustrates how your silhouette will show up also against the light background of the buildings.

Background and shadow

37. Against a dark background the light may reveal your shape.

Plate 32 (War—France)

For this reason never lean out of windows. Use the contained shadow.

Plate 33

38. Keep well back in the shadow. You can observe just as well from within.

Plate 34 (War—Normandy—Caen)

This sniper has a telescopic sight. The enemy sniper may have similar equipment.

The curtains are in place.

The dying foliage is out of place.

Therefore use materials which are not incongruous and close the window.

Shine

39. Your skin can reveal you by its tendency to shine.

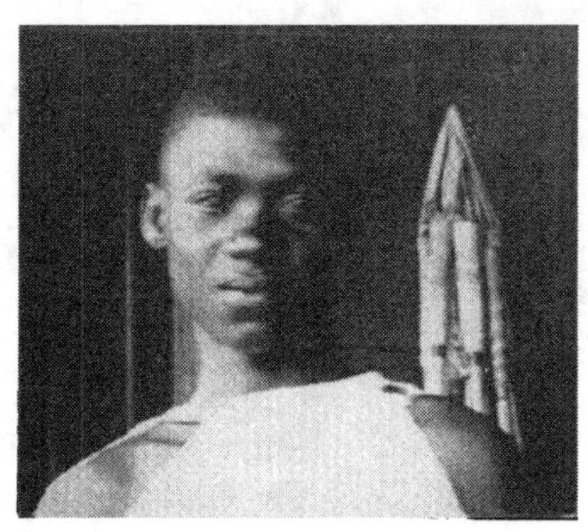

Plate 35 (Meru—Kenya)

Even where colour matches its surroundings there can be no concealment if there is shine.

Clothing and Equipment

40. Metal on equipment should be dulled and web equipment darkened to subdue shine.

Plate 36

Plate 37 (War—Normandy—St Mauvieu)

An example of clothing and equipment blending into the background.

41. When the clothing and equipment are coloured and toned down to match the surroundings, always move into the shade before you handle anything that may shine.

Plate 38 (Operations—Malaya)

A patrol commander and his guide, both dressed in 'jungle green', consulting a map in the shade.

SECTION 5—Use of sunlight and shadow

Soft sunlight

42. In temperate zones sunlight produces quieter tones and textures into which clothing and equipment will merge.

Plate 39 (War—Normandy)

MAKE USE OF NATURAL COVER.

Strong sunlight

43. In tropical countries the intense contrast between bright reflections and the shadows aids concealment.

Plate 40 (War—New Guinea—1942)

This soldier blends into his background.

Bright surfaces

44. Flat surfaces show every shadow, reveal every outline and reflect light. Shadows break up outlines.

Plate 41 (Canada)

This soldier flattens his body to suppress his own shadow and uses the broken shadows cast by the branches of the tree to help him to hide on the snow. In the picture opposite, brightness draws attention away from the shade. In this picture shade misleads the eye.

Concealment by linking

Plate 42

45. By linking up his outlines with the larger shapes and shadows of the twin tree trunks the sniper's shape is merged into the background.

46. Shapes, clothing and shadows blend with their surroundings when correctly sited.

Plate 43

Shapes, clothing and kits clash with their surroundings when incorrectly sited.

Plate 44

Observe how a head shows against the skyline. In both pictures there is good concealment in front of the skyline, but not on it.

Movement

47. Follow the lines of either the natural ground formation or along man-made boundaries such as walls, hedges and crop divisions.

Move by bounds. Keep still between bounds.

Plate 45 (War—Normandy) Clearing a Farm of snipers

In tone with their background although in the light, this section relies on their immobility to keep them unobserved while they plan their next bound.

48. When you move—move with speed and decision.

Plate 46 (War—Normandy) Beneath the sniper's window

The same section, having picked a good line of advance, the shelter of the wall, move with speed to the next bound.

Risks from reflections

49. Rivers, wet roads and such surfaces are like mirrors. They reveal by reflection when the background may seem to conceal.

Plate 47 (Jubbalpore, India)

The members of this platoon are almost invisible as they march across the bridge. They merge well with the background, but their reflections appear clear cut in the mirror the river provides. Reflections may reveal a patrol from across water by night when they are otherwise unseen.

Garnishing

50. Use the garnish from your immediate surroundings and make intelligent use of sunlight and shadow.

Plate 48 (War—Normandy)

51. Trucks, men, vehicles and a Bofors LAA gun. Shadows are often more readily recognizable than the equipments that cast them.

Plate 49

Troops on the march

52. Infantry on the march cast shadows easily recognizable from the air.

Plate 50 (War—Germany)

These soldiers shapes merge into the hedge shadow but their shadows show up on the road and identify them as marching troops.

Contained shadow

53. In this example no effort has been made to break up or conceal the internal shadows cast by the slit trenches. Remember shadow will reveal your position to the reconnaissance pilot.

Plate 51

CHAPTER 4—PRINCIPLES OF CONCEALMENT—UNIT AND SUB-UNITS

SECTION 7—Basic factors

54. This pamphlet so far has dealt mainly with the concealment of the individual and his weapon. This section will deal with collective concealment of groups and units. At other than close range the individual ceases to be of significant importance. He becomes a means by which positions, weapons and supplies can be located.

Plate 52 (Training—England)

The three figures standing in the open at the upper right centre of this scene arouse suspicion and reveal the 25 prs concealed under nets among the scrub.

Movement

Plate 53 (War—Korea)

55. The crest of the ridge offers easier going for these troops, but it makes them stand out against the sky. The key men and weapons can be picked out easily.

Shape

Plate 54 (War—Korea)

56. This tank would be less apparent had the commander sited it alongside one of the huts, as in the case of the other tank.

Shadows

57. Shadows are often more easily recognizable than the shapes that cast them.

Plate 55

This photograph reveals the location of a troop of self-propelled guns.

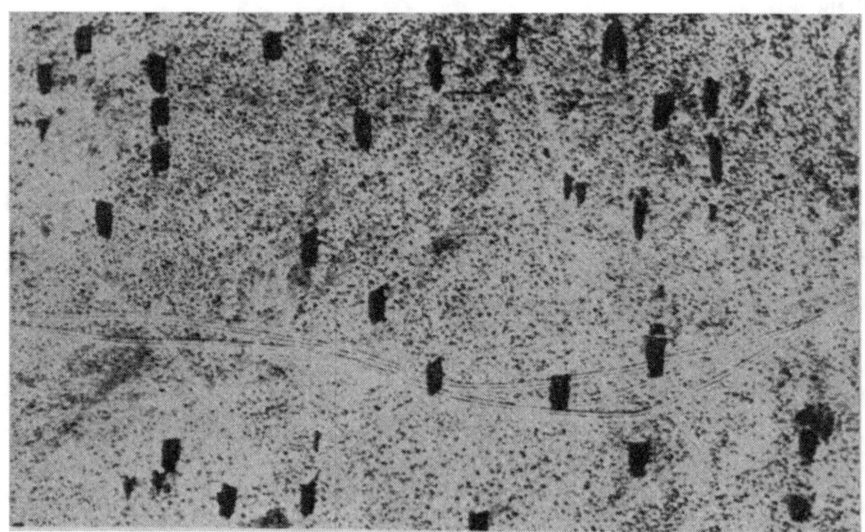

Plate 56

58. In colour and tone these vehicles match the Libyan desert so well that they should be almost invisible, but the hard black shadows cast by each vehicle allow an easy count to be made.

59. When sited out in the open, or under desert conditions, shadows must be avoided. To achieve this, lighter tones and uniform textures are used to merge objects into the terrain.

Plate 57 (War—Libya)

This illustrates how a man standing in the open can give away the location of his section and platoon position. Even so a careful look is needed to detect the weapon pit beside which he stands.

Tracks across different ground textures

Plate 58

60. In the above illustration, vehicle tracks across the cultivated area show white against the ground pattern; had the vehicle followed the line of the furrows the tracks made would have been less obvious and might well have been overlooked.

SECTION 8—Ground features and formation

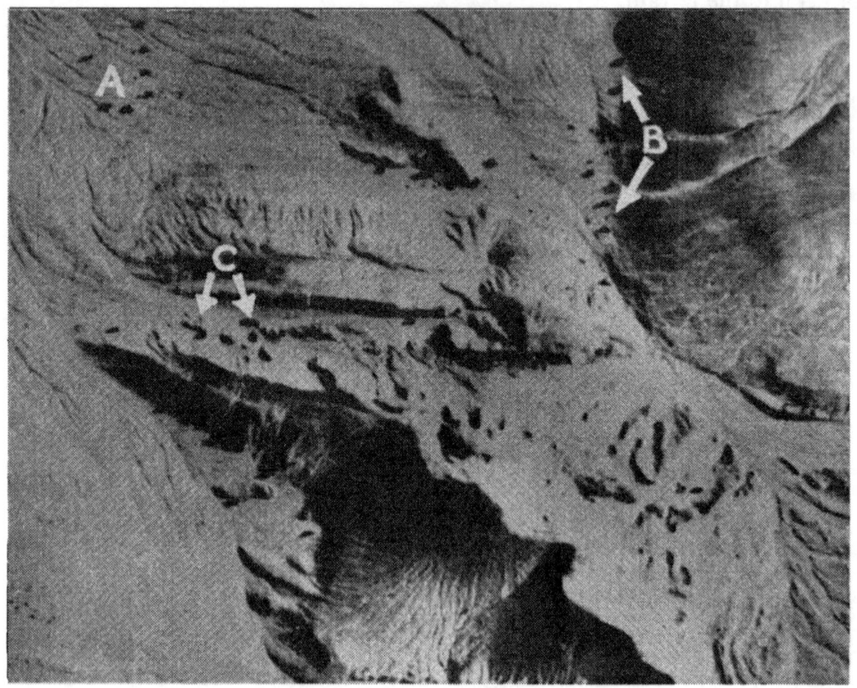

Plate 59 (War—Libya)

61. The Libyan desert is an example of terrain with little natural cover.

The vehicles badly sited at (A) stand out in unnatural contrast to the ground trends and shadows.

The vehicles at (B) have halted where large boulders and clumps of scrub are usual features. They are not easy to distinguish from these objects.

The vehicles at (C) have to be indicated. The sites selected blend in with the trend and shadows of the natural ground formation.

Thus by observation and adaptability it is possible to site so as to merge in with the hillsides, desert features and shadows although the ground itself is bare.

Towns and villages

62. In normal conditions, hamlets, small towns and other built over areas are the scenes of constant activities with resultant ground wear and patterns.

They usually are a focus of intricate road and path systems that are already well marked on the ground.

Military dispositions can be fitted into this pattern without fresh markings or disturbances. Keep the military vehicles and equipment concealed and avoid movement on the open roads.

The normal activities of village life do not disclose any signs of military occupation until we notice the badly sited vehicle in the courtyard. (Right foreground). This rouses suspicion and reveals probable military activity which may well be disclosed by subsequent photographic interpretation.

Plate 60

A   Badly sited vehicle in courtyard.

B   Large bushes or trees are not allowed to grow in farmyards. Here a large equipment-either tank, vehicle, or gun is simulated as a bush.

Plate 61. (Training—BAOŘ) Bad siting

63. In towns and villages, concealment can be obtained by siting alone. The net, foliage and the softer effects used in the countryside are replaced by blending in with shapes of buildings and the construction of disguises from building materials taken from the immediate surroundings.

Air observation reveals a unit or formation's vehicles parked in a small town's streets; in this case this offers no real concealment and may lead to dangerous traffic congestion. Vehicles must be moved clear of the streets without delay.

The approaches and surrounds of towns and villages usually offer better concealment than within built up areas.

Plate 62. (Training—BAOR)—Good siting.

64. A good example of the many aids to concealment a village offers.

Although the village was occupied by troops all vehicles were parked off the road and troops kept within cover.

Only a garage door (centre) left carelessly open revealed a military vehicle within. Then the Army truck under the tree beside it was noted.

That is how concealment is broken.

Plate 63 (Summer)

65. The villages and hamlets of the countryside of NW EUROPE provide a pattern in which it is easy to hide, especially in the summer when trees and hedges are in full leaf.

Plate 64 (Winter)

66. Trees cast leaves and vegetation wilts, crops are cut and fields ploughed. However, good concealment can still be found.

The day is short and at 1100 hours, when this photograph was taken, the low winter sun creates shadow patterns across the ground.

Woodlands

67. Woods offer good cover from observation, but good siting is necessary to obtain the maximum effect.

Plate 65.

In the illustration above the trees are sparse on the ground and the bright sunlight produces good shadow cover but the concealment is bad. More use could have been made of existing shadow and of natural foliage to conceal the position from aerial observation. Camouflage nets are conspicuous by their absence.

68. Wooded country may give indifferent cover from low altitude air observation. Dull light reduces the cover afforded by strong-shadows.

Plate 66

Troops in wooded areas often gain a false sense of security, concealment discipline often becomes lax when using rides and clearings and their movement. attracts low flying aircraft.

Rain

69. One's natural reaction is to get into shelter out of the rain. But heavy rain with its attendant low cloud gives good concealment while it lasts. Be alert to take advantage of this cover for movement and changes of site which can be carried out while enemy observation is restricted.

Plate 67

Dust

70. Dust can be a major problem in certain countries and may be seen from miles away. This heavy blast cloud is the dusty aftermath of only two rounds fired by artillery. This may be avoided by good siting.

Plate 68 (Nowshera—Pakistan)

CHAPTER 5—ARTIFICIAL AIDS TO CONCEALMENT

SECTION 9—Personal aids

71. There are a number of artificial aids which are available for use by the individual to help conceal himself. These are:—

(a) Helmet net and cover.

(b) Camouflage face cream.

(c) The face veil.

Plate 69

72. *(a) The helmet net*
Keep the steel helmet covered with the helmet net. Use garnish that matches your background.

(b) Camouflage cream
Apply camouflage cream to the exposed portions of the skin.

(c) The veil
This can be used to conceal the outline of the head and shoulders. Do not neglect minor points such as light linings, medal ribbons, buckles and buttons which reflect light.

SECTION 10—The camouflage net

73. Nets are used to help conceal regular shapes, shine and shadow of man-made equipments.

The net itself requires thickening with strips of fabric threaded through the mesh of the net. These are called garnish. *See* Diagram 1 (page 45). Without garnish the net will allow the object to show through, but the garnish must be applied in such a way that the net will not appear artificial or unnatural. The essentials are:—

(a) The outline of the net must be natural.

(b) The colour and texture of the garnish must blend with the background.

(c) The net must not cast hard artificial shadows.

Plate 70

74. The equipment concealed beneath the camouflage net cannot be identified because:

(a) The net is propped clear of the object.

(b) The garnish is sufficiently dense.

It will be seen that the outline of the net is irregular. Light penetrates the net, but the shadow cast is indistinct.

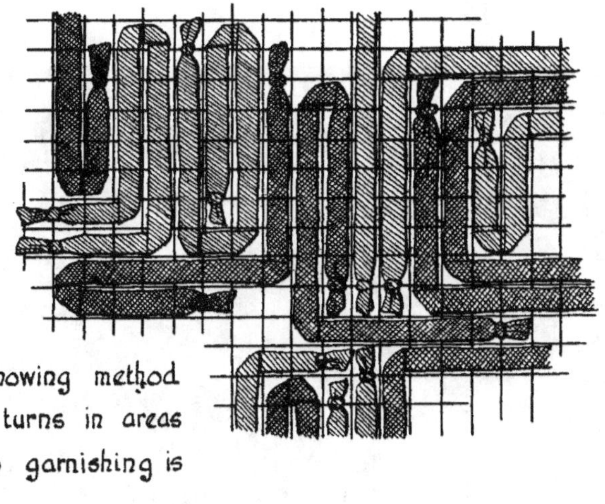

Above -
Diagram showing method
of making turns in areas
where strip garnishing is
used

Diagram 1

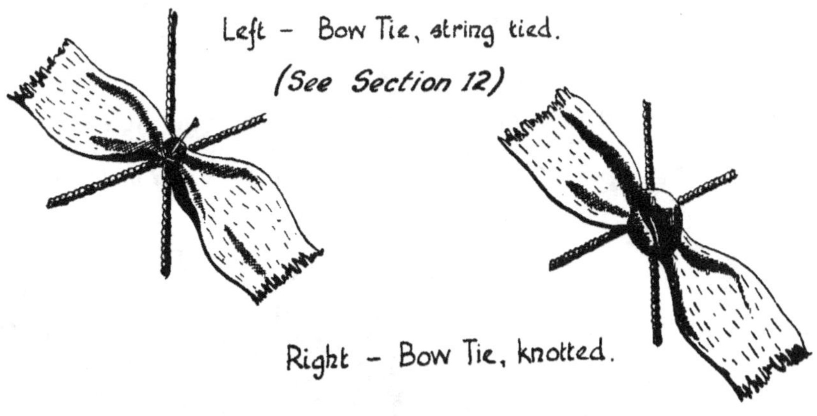

Left – Bow Tie, string tied.
(See Section 12)

Right – Bow Tie, knotted.

Diagram 2

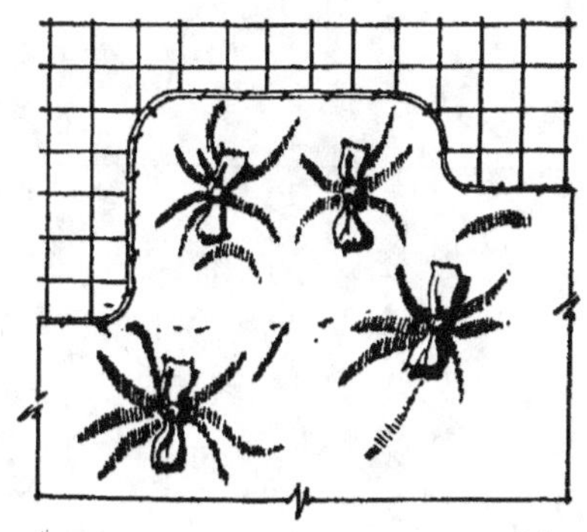

Left – Patch and Bow
Tie method.
(See Section 12)

Diagram 3

Garnish reflects light

Plate 71

75. The irregular pattern of the strips of garnish distract the eye and prevent it from identifying the equipment which it hides.

The net should not be over garnished or the concealment may be neutralised.

Foliage as a garnish

Plate 72

(Training—England)

76. In addition to artificial garnish (scrim), use may be made of foliage to help blend with the immediate surroundings. Keep such branches at their natural angle of growth and if possible train the living foliage across the net. Cut foliage should not be used in a position which is likely to be occupied for some time. Remember that any cut branches will wilt and will require changing. Avoid damage to foliage in your immediate vicinity.

Plate 73 (War—Italy)

Here five vehicles are concealed by training the natural foliage over the road.

77. If the net is used to cover a field work, grass can be used as garnish, but it will require frequent changing.

Garnish—Disruptive shadows

Plate 74

78. This is a picture of a sunken road completely covered over with the net used as a FLAT TOP. The comparatively thin garnishing breaks up the light and casts confusing shadow on the vehicle. The net must blend with the background, otherwise it will indicate that there is something concealed.

Use as a drape

Plate 75

79. An example of nets used as a " drape ". This is particularly effective as the nets hang in the shadow cast by the trees. It is in this shadow that the vehicles are concealed.

Flat top

Plate 76 (Training—England)

80. A flat top used to simulate the ground pattern. Here the net needs extra garnish to blend with the ground pattern. In making use of this " flat-top " method always have the garnishing clear of the edges of the netting.

Use of the net in open country

Plate 77

81. This wireless vehicle is well netted into a form that merges well with the surroundings.

Away from any cover the net is still of value if the site is chosen to conform to the ground pattern.

An example of aids badly applied

Plate 78

82. The errors in the above illustration are:—

    (a) Camouflage nets not propped away from the equipment, thus identifying it.

    (b) The garnish in the nets is inadequate.

    (c) No attempt has been made to cover the shining surfaces such as windscreens and headlights.

SECTION 11—**The collective use of the camouflage net**

83. It is often an advantage to collect the nets from a number of the vehicles or weapons in a unit and join these together, or use them " collectively " to make up a fairly large and spacious concealment scheme.

However, such collective use of nets must never deny a net to any weapon or vehicle which may be sent off to a task in some exposed site.

Plate 79 (War—Germany—1945)

84. A very good example of the intelligent use of nets.

The orchard trees give additional overhead cover and the full use of the hedge ties into the ground pattern. The road gives a good approach to this collective shelter. This is unlikely to be detected even at quite low levels.

Plate 80 (War—Italy)

85. This interior view of another collective example reveals the space and access to vehicles that good collective use may provide under the nets. The method of support is also clear.

86. Below is a good example of the use of a combination of nets used in an irregular pattern in open country. The nets are supported by posts and frames and allow ample room for the weapons to be fought from this concealed position without creating too obvious a feature on the ground.

Plate 81

87. Some suggestions are given in Diagram 4 for the collective use of nets stretched flat, ie, FLAT TOP to provide concealment within enclosures where they can be tied in with the boundary features.

Diagram 4

Collective use of the net—flat top

(A) Tied in with the hedges to stretch over a corner of a field with a covered entrance way. Method of support is shown.

(B) Stretched and garnished as a lean-to roof against a building.

(C) Stretched to form a false floor to a farmyard, or other roofless area within buildings.

(D) Tied across a garden or vegetable patch to indicate cultivation, while concealing stores etc hidden beneath it.

(E) On a site adjoining a roadway to provide a concealed park for vehicles. Note the tendency to sag which often spoils the effect.

(F) A frequent mistake. By adding side walls to a flat stretched net, it becomes an odd solid shape which fails to merge with the surroundings.

(G) Stretched between hedges to form a false road surface above the real one. When the ' flat top ' net is used, the open side must be as close to the ground as possible, or a low flying aircraft may discover its purpose.

SECTION 12—**Patch garnished nets**

88. For some purposes it is useful to have nets garnished with relatively large patches of material, such as canvas or hessian sack cloth, instead of with the more usual threaded strips. Such nets are called patch garnished or patch nets. Two types are held ready made for issue from Ordnance stocks:—

(a) The snow patch net.

(b) Artillery " patch and bow tie " nets.

89. Improvised patch garnishing, applied to standard nets, can be usefully employed. For example, where the surroundings present large patches of reflecting surfaces or hard blocks of light and deep shadow, it may help concealment to apply white, or black, or drab coloured fabric patches to the nets to merge with these local features. These conditions may occur among buildings, in rocky places, among the debris of bomb and shell damage in built-up areas and at times of light snow-fall.

Any form of patch cover must be very firmly fastened to the net, or wind and blast may blow it away.

Snow—patch—net

90. This is the issue pattern of the snow net. As an alternative, a plain sheet of calico material may be used.

The large white patches reproduce the patchy effect of light and shade. They also break up the shape of objects that might otherwise appear in black silhouette against the white snow on the ground under the net.

Improvised white patches on the darker " woodland " net are also effective.

Plate 82 (War—Holland)

In this illustration failure to cover the muzzle compromises this attempt at concealment.

Built-up areas

91. In built-up areas patch nets can also be improvised for use among the hard outlines and surfaces of buildings either demolished or intact. The patches may be gathered from local materials available on the site.

Plate 83

This picture shows a good example of this use, supplemented with some local garnish, in a damaged town.

Rock strewn areas

Plate 84

92. The entrance to a headquarters dug into a rocky hillside is screened by netting carrying large patches to simulate the rocky nature of the surroundings.

It was realised that the deep patches of shade are as important as those of shine, so the net was left free of any minor garnish with good effect.

Patch and bow-tie garnishing

93. This method of garnish is used for artillery camouflage nets because the bow-tie is more resistant to blast than strip garnish pattern. It is used to keep large patches in position. *See* diagrams 2 and 3 (page 45).

Plate 85 (Training—Australia)

94. An AA gun is dug into the hillside in the foreground. It is hidden beneath a net with a quick release device to unmask it for instant action.

The natural grass patch and scrub leaf effects combine well with the artificial patch and bow-tie so that the real is hard to separate from the false.

SECTION 13—The desert problem

95. In deserts the nets used must be large enough to cover an object fully and to flow down to the surrounding ground, thus merging all shapes and shadows with the ground surface.

There are two types of camouflage nets for use in desert areas:—

(a) For uniform sand coloured areas the " net lightweight road coloured material " or Raschel net is employed.

(b) In broken country with sandstone outcrop the " net, garnished, desert ", is used. This net is garnished with white, sand-coloured and pink strip.

The Raschel net

96. The Raschel net is a close mesh woven cotton material and is opaque when viewed from the air. This hides the shine and shadow of the concealed object. The Raschel material is supported on an 8 inch rectangular mesh net which may be used to carry additional garnish when required, eg, scrub or dark cloth patches in appropriate areas.

Plate 86 (Training—Egypt)

97. *RASCHEL NETS IN USE.* Although the Raschel net blends well with the bare ground, the slightly raised edges show as black lines of shadow. The netted shapes also cut across the flow pattern of the dry runnels in the sand. The edges of the net should touch the ground.

More careful siting and the addition of small clumps of the scrub as garnish could improve the concealment in this desert example.

SECTION 14—The spider

98. The spider is an artificial aid made with thick wire and steel wire wool for the concealment of MMG positions and is only available for this purpose.

Plate 87 (Training—England)

99. When well sited in suitable surroundings, as here, it gives excellent concealment without additional garnish.

Plate 88

100. The same Spider illustrating the lightness and ease of removal. The machine gun was able to fire effectively from the cover.

SECTION 15—**Other camouflage materials available as ordnance issues**

(Listed in Appendix B)

101. Hessian sheet

The sheets are issued in two colours, brown or green. The size of each sheet is 12 ft × 20 ft.

Hessian sheet is useful as ground covering, for making patch nets and for covering up specially shiny surfaces such as windscreens.

102. Coir screens

These are for use when more solid effects are needed to imitate portions of masonry and other man made structures.

They are issued in two sizes:—   12 ft × 48 ft; 6 ft × 24 ft

They are painted on both sides either in brown or in green.

103. Steel wire wool

This valuable aid consists of steel wool coated with a rust preventative and painted. It can produce an excellent simulation of plough, grass, and similar textures and can tone in with natural surroundings even in the open. It is supplied in rolls 2 yards wide by 25 yards long mounted on a base of galvanized wire netting in two colours; grass green or earth brown.

104. Steel wire wool is tougher and more enduring than natural materials and is easy to install on many sites, but it is somewhat bulky and inflexible. For this reason it is usually best employed to help camouflage defence works and fixed objects or sites. Below, however, it is used to cover a headquarters and its vehicles and has produced a good simulation of grass banking.

Plate 89 (Training—BAOR—Germany)

105. The standard net itself is made of jute twine in a 3-inch square mesh.

New types now coming into service are of a material which will be fire, water and rot proof.

106. The garnishing material is made of coloured hessian (obsolescent) or a plastic material called PVC which has replaced hessian garnish. PVC's advantages are that it is non-absorbent and non-inflammable.

107. A list of the more important sizes of standard nets is shown at Appendix A. These nets, ready garnished, are available in Ordnance stocks for issue to units in accordance with current camouflage equipment scales.

Care of nets

108. After use, all types of nets should be correctly folded after removal of foliage (*see* diagram 5, page 59). They must not be stored unless thoroughly dry.

When in store they should be inspected at least once every three months and any necessary repairs effected. Hessian nets must not be stored near POL or paint.

Re-garnishing

109. After a time in use a net will require re-garnishing. This is a unit responsibility.

CARE OF CAMOUFLAGE NETS: Correct method of folding

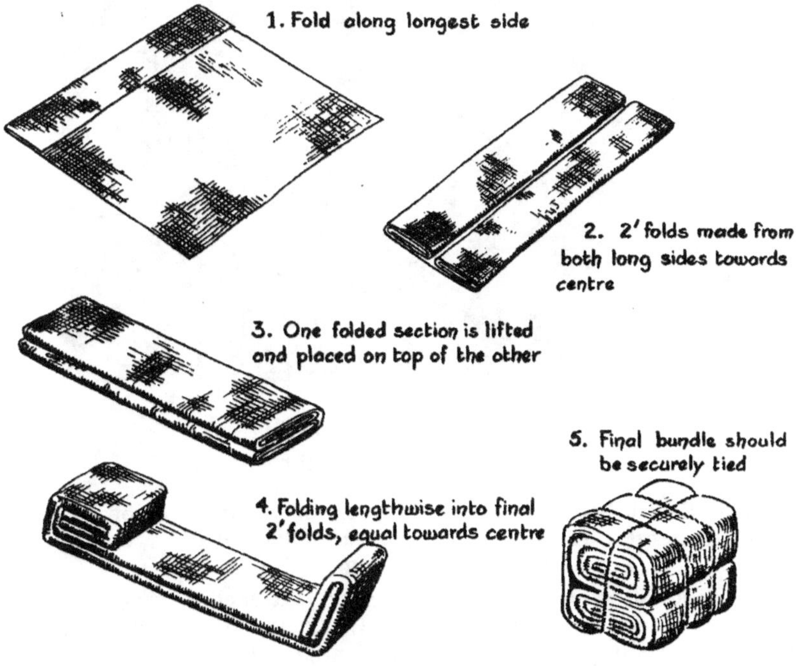

Diagram 5

CHAPTER 6—CONCEALMENT OF INFANTRY AND THEIR WEAPONS

SECTION 17—General

110. Infantry, perhaps above all other arms, must know how to conceal themselves from ground and air observation.

    (a) Ground observation. Most modern armies possess highly trained observers; these observers are equipped with all modern aids including infra-red devices.

    (b) Air observation. The most common faults made by infantry in recent years, when endeavouring to conceal themselves from air observation, are:—

        (i) Failure to visualize what the ground looks like from above.

        (ii) Failure to hide spoil and conceal weapon pits, equipment and tracks.

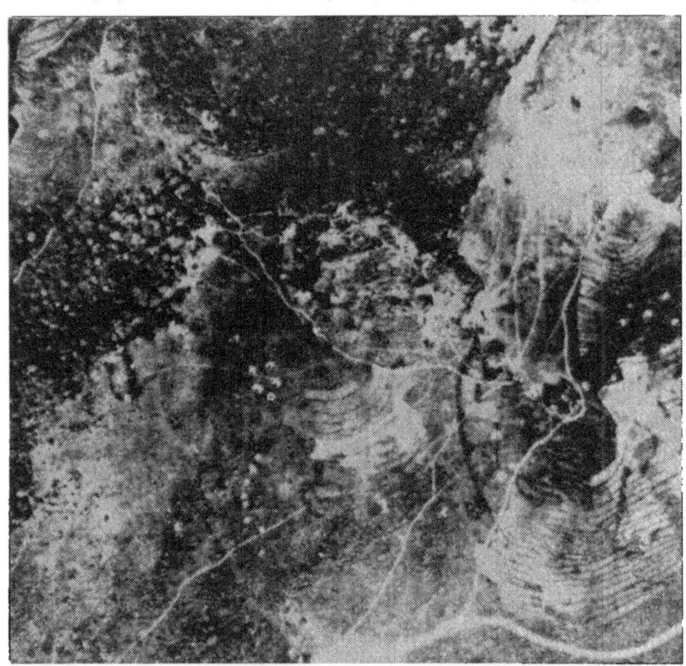

Plate 90 (War—Arakan—Burma)
An infantry position

111. This British battalion's position offers all the information an enemy air observer can desire. The unit locations, the individual posts, communications and bivouac areas are all pin-pointed for him.

There was no attempt to cover up the spoil of trench digging which outlines each post. The lack of track discipline and the heavy surface wear this has caused show that the position is of some size and importance and has probably been occupied for a number of days.

112. To know the exact positions of the defenders' forward posts greatly simplifies the attackers' plan.

Plate 91 (Training—England)

A platoon locality

This position needs:—

(a) Better siting within the ground pattern.
(b) Efforts to mask and conceal contained shadow in each pit.
(c) Concealment of spoil.

Preliminary reconnaissance

113. Movement and unnecessary tracks made during reconnaissance and the siting of a position, may indicate to the enemy points to watch.

The final reconnaissance of each site should be made on foot. The main track plan should be decided on at this stage.

Plate 92 (Training—BAOR)

This Infantry carrier is well tied in to the end of a large haystack while the final reconnaissance of an Infantry position is in progress.

Task planning

114. The plan and work for concealing a position must be done systematically.

    (a) Site your posts within the ground pattern.

    (b) Make a simple crawl trench plan following the same pattern.

    (c) Enforce this as the only track plan from the start.

    (d) Mark out each weapon pit. Work from within these marks.

    (e) Roll the turf and the weathered surface soil away from the pit on every side. Keep this free from dug out spoil.

    (f) Layer the spoil evenly around the pit as you dig it out.

    (g) Roll back the turf and replace the old surface dirt over the freshly dug spoil to hide it.

    (h) Remove any surplus spoil into cover nearby. Hide it along hedgerows, at the foot of trees or among debris.

    (j) Where trampling is unavoidable, disguise it afterwards.

115. There is no time to waste.

No relaxation is permissible before concealment measures are completed.

However sound the construction of a field work may be, it is weak if it can be seen or if air photography pinpointed its position while it was still under construction.

Plate 93 (War—Korea)

Siting

116. Site for surprise and protection.

Good fire positions are essential. Many defences are destroyed because the enemy is trained to look for obvious sites.

A second choice that gives concealment is preferable to an obvious site that invites destruction.

Plate 94 (War—Imphal—Burma)

This field of fire could have been covered as well from the background cover as from these breastworks built out in the marsh.

The enemy mortars could prevent the defenders firing a single shot

117. Site within the ground pattern.

If possible avoid making parapets. The ground level gives better protection and concealment   Fit your position into the existing pattern.

Plate 95

Plate 96 (War—Germany) Good siting

This LMG post fits neatly into the ground pattern. Its occupants leave no tracks on the hard approach behind it. It is screened from the air view. A more obvious site within the building will receive the fire it deserves.

Plate 97 (Training—Germany) Bad siting

These weapon pits were dug with no regard for ground pattern or texture. Corners of the crop diversions offer better sites and the vegetation would absorb spoil from the digging.

The track rings on the tillage draw attention to the trench. The piled spoil adds shadow to the shine.

Overhead cover

118. The trench itself shows as an open dark shadow when viewed from above. Overhead cover can eliminate this feature, as well as giving some physical protection. It can be provided in three forms:—

    (a) Light frame lids merely to conceal. These offer no protection and are designed to be thrown off to engage the enemy.

    (b) Trench shelters to provide overhead protection (OHP) alongside the fire position within the same pit. This offers concealment and protection from the splinter effects of low air burst shelling. This shelter is made with its roof level flush with the ground. It aids concealment.

    (c) Emplacement overhead protection to provide protection from solid missile and blast, and cover from beneath which a weapon can fire. This type of OHP protrudes above the ground level of the weapon it covers. It makes a concealment problem.

119. When turf is not available, artificial materials can be used to match the natural ground surface.

Plate 98 (War—Italy)

These light well garnished covers match the surface on which they rest. Flush with the ground they are inconspicious themselves and conceal the pits they cover. They provide no target.

120. Heavy overhead cover from beneath which the riflemen and the machine gunners can fire tends to create too many structures to conceal.

Plate 99 (Training—England)

This overhead cover may be splinter proof but the hard outline over the dark shadow is made worse by the light that outlines the soldiers heads. The desire to gain all round observation creates this risk.

Plate 100 (Training—England)

121. This section post is part of a platoon position made with strong overhead cover to resist the effects of atomic blast and radiation as well as heavy mortar attack.

It is obvious and invites destruction in its unconcealed state.

Plate 101

The same area after careful concealment with turf and grass tufts resembles an outcrop in rough ground.

But such concealment must be secure and attached to the object it covers. Light grass and similar loose materials can be washed or blown away by rain or wind.

122. Do not think only in terms of turf for concealment; it is not always available. Dig round and preserve any leafy vegetation that offers concealment. Re-plant if necessary.

Plate 102

This weapon pit shares the shade for the bush and so resembles a patch of fallen leaves. The taller clumps of grass remain undisturbed to produce concealment for the LM gunner's head and shoulders.

123. Adapt yourself to natural sites.

Plate 103

Fallen tree trunks are usually near woods. Here this natural feature is used to disguise a weapon. The garnish of light branches assist disguise by softening the shadow of the weapon slits.

A section post position

124. A two-man weapon pit in turf on chalk soil.

Plate 104 (Training—England)

When dug, all the white chalk spoil was removed and the two man slit made flush with the ground. Dark hessian is used to screen the white subsoil.

Plate 105 The section's three pits

Each pit has overhead cover and is almost invisible when viewed from a bank only a few yards away.

125. The same type of two-man pit with a light frame of wood with wire mesh and local garnish to cover the opening.

Plate 106 (Training—England)

There is a complete absence of any mound.

Plate 107 (Training—England)

When the flap is down the weapon pit becomes unnoticeable at twenty yards.

Concealment in the desert

126. Until it has weathered for some time, newly dug spoil may differ in colour and texture from surface sand and gravel.

But, in general, the use of raschel or hessian combined with surface soil can give good concealment.

Plate 108 (War—Libya)

Here a platoon position covered with wire frames and staked wires to support dyed hessian covers achieves complete concealment while inactive. It was necessary to tape its location to prevent accidents.

Concealment in the jungle

127. In jungle country, concealment of weapon pits is an easy matter. The Japanese were expert at digging without disturbance. Many of their works were carried out within a few yards of British positions without being heard. The natural growth of the vegetation was untouched. The spoil was removed with great patience and the results justified their labour.

Plate 109

(War—Burma—Imphal) A sniper's fox-hole alongside the gun with spent rounds on the front edge.

Plate 110

(War—Burma—Imphal)

128. A typical Japanese fire position.

A normal two-man weapon slit occupied by one man.

Two-thirds of the opening roofed by logs and earth with subsoil and turfs replaced and growing.

The firer looks out from the two-foot square opening and can throw grenades or jump out easily.

129. Bunkers for LMGs or two or three riflemen about 6 feet square, sunk completely underground and with complete overhead cover. A six-inch fire slit with the lintel log supported on Y shaped uprights. Roofing logs, six-inches in diameter; uncovered to show construction.

Plate 111

(War—Burma—Imphal)

The fire slit raised six inches and a six-inch elbow rest dug behind dyed hessian sand-bags gives ample clearance for the weapon.

Plate 112

(War—Burma—Imphal)

The same after replacement of soil and vegetation.
Note the undamaged growth of the foliage growing to conceal the fire-slit.
Its value is well worth the care.

Plate 113 (War—Burma—Imphal)

A well concealed post

130. The Japanese bunker thirty yards away was not visible until within ten yards distance. The net which concealed the narrow loophole at ground level has been pulled away for this photograph.

Thick overhead cover with logs and spoil were covered with growing foliage and each bunker covered the next one.

In one case the track was continued over the top of a bunker.

131. Communication crawl trenches should follow the natural trends as closely as possible.

Plate 114 (War—Burma—Imphal)

The communication trench leaves the bunker on the left, twists round a bush, passes another bunker entrance just visible beyond the bush and enters a third bunker behind the bush.

SECTION 18—Personal and platoon weapons and equipment

132. The previous section was concerned with the concealment of the sub-unit and the individual soldier in a variety of surroundings This section deals with the concealment of infantry weapons and equipment.

133. This presents three main concealment problems:—

(a) Methods of keeping weapons concealed so that they cannot be observed or associated with any particular arm.

(b) Disguising the special characteristics of their fire power.

(c) Movement associated with replenishment of ammunition, etc.

134. Distinctive weapons, clothing and equipment, eg, binoculars and map cases may indicate the commander in a unit or sub-unit. These features must be disguised in the field. This also applies to such equipment as wireless sets, range finders, etc.

The light machine gun

Plate 115 (War—Imphal Burma)
Be a good shot and a bad target

135. Within a hundred yards of the enemy, by keeping low and aiming round
the side of his cover, this light machine gunner increases his chances of killing
his enemy without being seen. His concealment would be assisted by the use of
a helmet net.

Plate 116 (War—Normandy)
An easy target

136. The LMG is the main fire power of the section but any tendency to bunch
around it invites retaliation on to the one spot.

The posting of the remainder of the section at different view-points to that
of the section commander and the LM gunner not only gives greater protection
but also increases the chances of locating concealed enemies.

137. *The risks of parapets.* The bipod gives a good ground clearance to the gun. Keep the gun as low as possible and provide side and background cover for its position from the spoil. Cover or remove all spoil from digging.

Plate 117 (War —Normandy)

With hastily dug weapon pits the desire to increase the field of fire tends to mount the LMG high on a parapet; above which the head and shoulders of the gunner, as well as his gun, will project.

Plate 118 (War—Normandy)

138. *Guard against dust.* Disclosure by dust. Foresee this risk before the enemy sees its result. This advice applies to every fire position.

The Ack Pack (Flame Thrower Portable No. 5)

Plate 119 The Ack Pack's garnished net cover

139. As a flame can achieve decisive effects on resistance from bunkers and similar strong points, the Ack Pack operator is a priority target for the enemy defenders.

As the flame-thrower has very limited range its operator has to get close to the target before using it and special camouflage is necessary to disguise the equipment.

This camouflage net cover for the Ack Pack is in position on the leading man in this picture; it has a quick release in case of entanglement.

The 2 inch Mortar

140. The mortar is not easy to conceal due to its high angle of fire, making overhead cover difficult, its bulky ammunition and the smoke it produces on firing.

Plate 120 (War—Italy)

Keep the mortar beneath cover. Do not leave bomb cases on the parapet.

Plate 121 (War—Belgium)

The mortar position is revealed by movement.

Plate 122

A dark background will show the mortar smoke so avoid this if possible.

Wireless communication

141. The concealment of the Man-Pack wireless set is essential, as it presents a priority target.

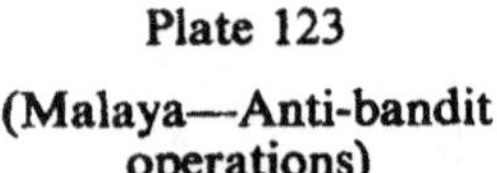

Plate 123

(Malaya—Anti-bandit operations)

This operator realises that the box like shape of his wireless set may indicate the importance of the site, so he places it where the light and shadow in the undergrowth will break up its typical outline.

SECTION 19—The medium machine gun

The medium machine gun

142. As the capacity for sustained fire is a characteristic of the medium machine gun, the concealment of the MMG post requires two considerations:—

(a) To provide complete disguise when silent.

(b) To offer a poor target while firing.

Plate 124 (War—India) Cast shadow

143. This soldier makes good use of the shine and shadow of the scrub in the bright Indian sunlight to break up the outlines of the machine gun and of himself.

Plate 125 (War—Belgium)

144. Sustained fire tends to produce a great deal of dust and unless the ground in front of the gun has been well chosen and prepared, the effects of blast may give the position away. Here we not only see this dust but also a complete lack of effort to conceal.

145. Strong overhead cover is needed for a machine gun post. Concealment is also essential.

Plate 126 (War—Belgium)

Disregard for the litter you produce in battle may give the enemy the exact location.

Plate 127 (War—River Senio—Italy)

146. Do not construct your post so that you provide a " Bulls eye " for the enemy's aim.

The machine gunner has to expose his head and shoulders as he sits behind the gun. So give him a good background and do not make either the post itself or the opening too obvious.

Plate 128 Contained shadow

147. This MMG post is well sited to match its surroundings, but the shadow contained by the shelter appears dark in comparison with the surrounding ground. The light from behind the shelter should have been screened to avoid outlining the shape of the gun.

Plate 129 (War—Libya) Use of local materials.

148. A machine gun post disguised as a heap of rubbish from the sugar cane plantation in the background.

The material used and the access track is normal to the site and would not arouse suspicion.

Plate 130 (Training—England) The machine gun section signature

149. This demonstration site came in for just criticism as it ignored concealment. Such a site would stand out in clear record for an air camera.

Note how the two guns and the section commander's post together make a rough " W " signature.

Plate 131 (War—Germany—Battle of Wesel) Mobile warfare

150. Amid the devastation of a captured enemy position, machine gunners endeavour to stem a counter attack.

The siting of the guns back from the crest is good.

The cover behind the guns allows ammunition supplies without revealing movement, but the typical " W " signature of the machine gun section appears again even here.

151. Use a good background to confuse the attacker as to the origin of the defensive fire.

Plate 132 (War—Libya)

This machine gun section post looks obvious on the hillside.

Plate 133 (War—Libya) " What a little camouflage will do ".

After a little treatment with dyed hessian, combined with the natural rocks around, it resembles any other out-crop of the rocky hillside.

152. This MG section post is constructed as a prolongation of a natural ground feature.

Plate 134 (War—Libya)

The dark gun slits and the vertical sandbagged walls show up and the tracks in the foreground also act as pointers to the site.

Plate 135 (War—Libya)

But after a little treatment these signs disappear and all that is seen is a typical piece of rough scrub common to the surrounding area.

The range finder

Plate 136 (Training—England)

153. Ranges are taken from new positions selected for the support weapons. Any carelessness on the part of the range-takers may indicate these positions to the enemy.

A range taker must use all the fieldcraft and care that a sniper uses in getting into and leaving his position.

SECTION 20—The 3 inch Mortar

Plate 137 (War—France)—The pit

154. Once a mortar opens fire it invites retaliation. A pit gives protection but, uncovered, it is easy to identify from the air owing to the shadow it contains.

Plate 138

155. This mortar can also engage the enemy with but little loss of concealment.

There is no parapet to ring the pit. It is flush with the ground, all spoil is removed and the net still gives protection by disguise.

156. "*Mortar signatures*".   One mortar pit may be overlooked but similar sites and pits nearby also attract attention.

Mortars require a collective plan for their section concealment.   Avoid lines and similarity of site.

Plate 139 (Training—England) An example of what can be done.

157. A section's mortar pits with a command post and ammunition pit dug and connected with crawl trenches between them.

The existing track in the foreground was used to transport all the spoil from the digging away from the site.   All surface scars returfed and shelters dug down to keep them flush with the ground level.   The returfed areas require watering to help prevent the grass withering.

The pegs mark the nearest pit.

Plate 140

The same pit with the net thrown back, as for firing.   The white chalk of the subsoil has been covered by a hessian lining to the pit.

The crawl trenches are covered with camouflage netting garnished with grass.

Such effective concealment gives surprise and denies the enemy a target to range on.

158. Mortars may reveal themselves by a characteristic " onion "-shaped flash above their cover.

Plate 141

(War—Italy)—Flash

Dull light and dark backgrounds can make this flash very obvious. The larger the mortar the more pronounced the flash, and the higher it is above the weapon. Check your site for background before you adopt it.

Flash can also reflect by night on tall features around the site. The appreciation of selecting the most suitable background for your weapon should be enphasized in training.

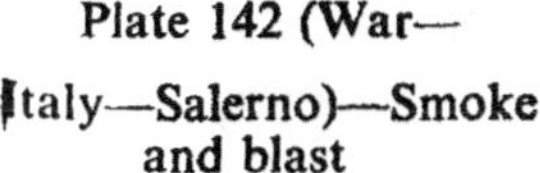

Plate 142 (War—

Italy—Salerno)—Smoke and blast

159. Although the smoke from one round is slight, it accumulates in still air. It is apparent among dark cover and vegetation.

Light overhead natural cover, as here, can offer a good shadow pattern but it is liable to show disturbance by blast as well.

Plate 143—Dust

160. Dusty sites are best avoided as dust does not dispel as readily as smoke. It is often more obvious from a distance than it may appear to be close at hand.

Damp or cover over bearing surfaces near the mortar before firing,

Plate 144 (War—Italy—Anzio)—Human activity and litter

161. Rapid fire is strenuous work and demands concentration on the job. But by discarding their shirts this crew has increased the risks of disclosure by movement. Unnecessary movement around the mortar pit should be avoided.

The mortar itself is small but the litter it creates can be large. Discarded bomb carriers accumulate rapidly in action, so plan their disposal into cover beforehand.

SECTION 21—The 120-mm BAT

162. The shape of the BAT is small and squat in size and painted the same basic colour as its surroundings. But the long smooth barrel and the flat metal surfaces of the shield catch the light and shine.

Plate 145

(Training—England)

Well sited and dug down in its pit, this BAT's position is inconspicuous from other angles but, where it catches the light, the metallic shine can indicate it from a long way off.

Plate 146 (Training—England)

By wrapping hessian along the barrel and erecting a low rigged net garnished with grass, the weapon is effectively concealed from all angles and from the air view.

This pit includes a small shelter and allows the ammunition, and the empty cases, to be kept hidden.

163. Separate command pits prevent overcrowding and activity near the gun, thereby revealing its position.

The ground before and behind the gun can be kept damp or otherwise covered to reduce dust from the blast discharge.

Plate 147 (Training—England)

164. This attempt at concealment of a 120-mm BAT was successful from the ground view at 200 yards but the damage and trampling caused in clearing the field of fire would have been fatal to concealment from the air. The barrel has been well countersunk into a depression in the ground dug for it, but the use of netting and wire wool has not concealed the outline of the shield.

The cut foliage although only recently applied, has already wilted. Its replacement would involve movement during daylight.

Plate 148—The same weapon from behind

165. The use of wire wool to mask the gun shield is the accepted practice for the BAT.

The damage to foliage and the dirt thrown up by the heavy back blast of the BAT when fired is a difficult problem. This may, to some extent, be overcome by careful siting and by keeping the ground immediately behind the gun damp or covered with hessian.

SECTION 22—Wire

166. Wire impedes normal movement and other ground activities. This often results in differences of texture between the fenced off areas and their surroundings. It also causes deviations in existing tracks to appear.

The wire fence does not cast much shadow in itself, however, grass and other vegetation grows rank beneath the fence which then appears to the air view as a darker textured band across the ground.

In desert, wire acts as a wind break which causes deposits of dust and rubbish to form beneath its fencing that mark it out to the air.

These effects appear after the fence has been up a few days but the tracks of construction and maintenance appear at the time of erection. Therefore, wire must closely follow the existing ground pattern to remain concealed.

Plate 149 (War—France)

This much enlarged photograph of a German strong point in France shows the concealment risks of wire in a static position.

Compare the ungrazed and untilled surfaces within the wire's perimeter with those outside. The traces of patrols also outline the wire fence. As the civilians cannot follow the main path their footsteps have created a new path in by-passing the defences on the right.

A strong point has become a well defined target.

167. A serious danger to tactical wiring in the open is that it can indicate defended localities although the other defences are well hidden.

Plate 150 (War—Germany) Recently erected wire

Only a dim shadow marks the wire across the landscape. But disregard for the farming pattern and the path trodden by its erectors, show the fence clearly to the air.

Wire should follow the normal ground pattern as closely as possible. A heavily wired hedgerow, the line of a bank, a roadside, or other usual divisions will not be obvious and will gain surprise.

Here the wire discloses a seemingly innocent farmstead as the site of a defended locality.

Low single strands of wire set out on stakes in triangular pattern are easy to conceal within grass or any other standing crop. Crops and scrub in general offer good concealment to loose wire and has the additional advantage of surprise.

The tight double apron fence is the most visible form from the air. Therefore, whenever possible, rely on reinforcing existing fixtures and netted obstacles in preference to creating an artificial line across the ground pattern.

SECTION 23—Anti-tank minefields

168. Hand-laid mines

Plate 151 (Training—BAOR)

In this case the dumping vehicles have tended to draw attention to the mined area with their tracks. If these mines had been dumped along the fence and thence manhandled into position the minefield would be far less obvious.

Plate 152

(Training—England)

169. This minefield reveals itself by an unnatural disregard for the field patterns. Across one field it might be mistaken for tillage but across three fields, its military signature is clear.

170. Mechanically laid mines

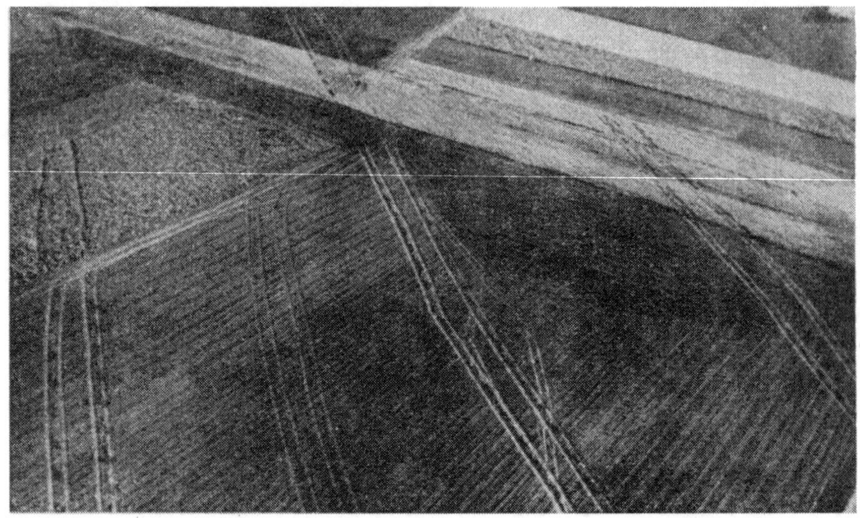

Plate 153

The track of the machine laid mine line is easy to identify. But there is no justification for such blatant disregard for the ground pattern as is displayed here. This is so obvious that the enemy would waste little time in penetrating it.

171. It is better to disguise the real by careful siting into background pattern, but when time permits, the use of dummy fields misleads the aerial observer.

Plate 154

(Training—England)

A little more care would have avoided the crude turning pattern. The placing may be technically correct, but these mines appear as an odd activity on the plough. Follow the farmer more closely; the extra " blind run " between the lines, would justify itself by closing the gap between farmer's work and soldiers'.

CHAPTER 7—THE CONCEALMENT OF WHEELED VEHICLES

SECTION 24—Track discipline

172. The " military signature " is mostly written in tracks. Weapons, equipment and even field works may be passed unnoticed if there are no track indications of activity.

173. The preoccupations of army life make men ignore the different pattern they are creating on the ground.

Even where track discipline exists, it is necessary to keep a check on wear.

This applies equally to pedestrian and to vehicle traffic.

Plate 155 (War—France) (German coastal defences)

Movement usually follows either straight or winding courses; it seldom takes sharp right angle turns.

A few well planned tracks would have reduced this welter of " short cuts ".

As it is, the marks of activities have drawn attack from the air as the bomb craters show.

SECTION 25—The problem of vehicle tracks and shape

174. The wheeled vehicle is the " maid of all work " of the army. It is the most numerous class of vehicle and the many tasks for which it is used entail a lot of movement. This may be in convoys or by single vehicles.

Although wheeled vehicles have a fair cross-country performance their main work is along roads and tracks. Therefore the main concealment problems arise on roads and in the control of tracks leading to and from roads.

Vehicles must follow existing tracks and keep as close to the existing ground pattern as possible.

Where existing tracks are in use, they may also require attention to disguise the effects of hard wear on their surfaces.

Military tasks may differ from civil and farming activities. The appearance of vehicles in unusual places often give enemy observers clear indications of what is going on behind our lines.

175. This snow carries on its texture the main problems that vehicle tracks create.

Plate 156

From right to left

(A)   Top right: a vehicle track driven straight across the open over an unused surface that readily reveals track markings on its soft texture.

(B)   Above the direct track: the marks of short sorties into softer texture made while manoeuvring into concealment sites.

(C)   The unconcealed resting by the concealed beyond the snow hummock. A fair attempt has been made to avoid giving the impression of this being a terminal point for a vehicle, by the track passing on beyond it.

(D)   Lack of track discipline has widened the tracked area unnecessarily.

(E)   A needless circuit out into the open that attracts the eye immediately.

(F)   A virtue; the track skirting the woodland edge pattern so closely that it might be overlooked by a fast travelling aircraft.

(G)   Tracks leading into unusual sites within woods. Use the woodcutters route and disperse when within.

(H)   Pedestrian footprints in a " short cut " across the open by the circuit.

Vehicle shape

Plate 157 (Training—BAOR)

176. Roofs and canopies accentuate the oblong shape of the chassis. These vehicle shapes make rectangular blocks which reflect shine and are hard to conceal amid natural cover although they do blend in with the formal patterns of built-up areas.

Plate 158

177. The flatness of the roof is too often ignored and the net is placed over the vehicle in this useless manner.

Shine

178. Sunlight reflects brilliantly from the glass windscreen and the headlamp reflectors.

This brilliant shine can give a vehicle's position away at many miles range from the observer.

It occurs both while on the move and while at rest. The crew of the vehicle may be quite unaware of the existence of this shine from their vehicle.

All reflectors, glass and metal work, must be covered as much as possible.

Plate 159 (Training—BAOR)

The glass surface of the windscreen and headlamps must be fully covered while the vehicle is at rest.

It is the first precaution after siting for concealment.

Site

Plate 160

179. When the concealment site is chosen first decide the angle and the position in which the vehicle is best concealed.

Do this with a minimum of manoeuvring on the site.

Contained shadow

Plate 161

180. Cover contained shadow by shutting the rear doors and closing the canopy. Avoid the dense blackness of contained shadow, even with the vehicle in shade.

Characteristic shapes

Plate 162

181. Cover and disguise the wheels and the shadows beneath the chassis.

Tie-in

Plate 163

182. Mount the net over the vehicle. Be careful to tie it into the nearby cover. Keep the net propped clear of the vehicle's shape.

SECTION 26—Choice of background and site

183. The wrong background can also disclose a vehicle that might otherwise pass unobserved.

Plate 164 (Training—Germany)

Watch for changes in shade and shadow. Where a parking site provides shade cover, an alternative site must be chosen in readiness for the time when the shadow alters with the position of the sun.

Lack of alertness to these changes of light often allows the enemy observer to confirm suspicions aroused in an earlier reconnaissance.

Foliage

184. The garnishing of vehicles with foliage is useful in the right place but it requires a lot of foliage to disguise the shape of a vehicle and remember that once the foliage has wilted it is useless.

It also tends to hamper the driver and reduce the efficiency of the vehicle in use.

Plate 165

In a wrong setting it only draws attention to itself.

Plate 166

Even where the foliage is appropriate to the background the vehicle must tie-in with it. Real bushes do not thrive on tarmac roads. These trucks should have parked further in.

Snow

185. Use of the snow net in changeable climates. The site selected should allow for the sudden changes that may follow a thaw.

Plate 167

This Jeep is sited under a snow net at a point where a snow drift might occur.

Plate 168

The site still offers concealment even after the snow net has been removed.

186. Out in the open snow even at close range, it is hard to recognise the darker part of this mound as a vehicle's shape and shadow.

Viewed down-sun, the effects of tracks and trampling in the snow are not very apparent:—

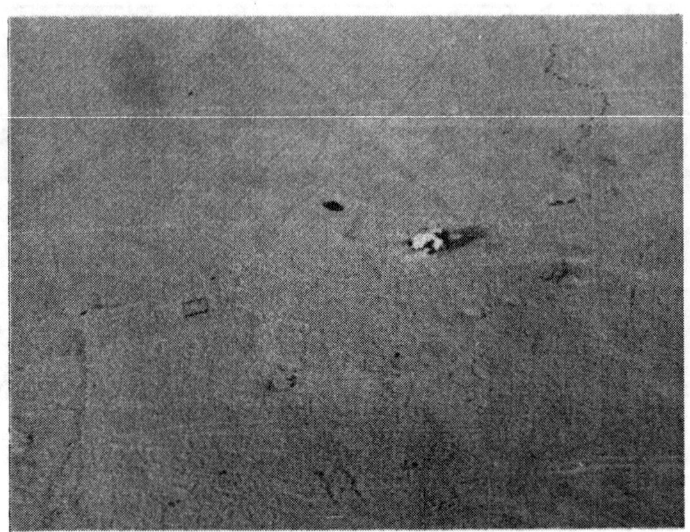

Plate 169

But when viewed across sun from the air, the track marking becomes very obvious.

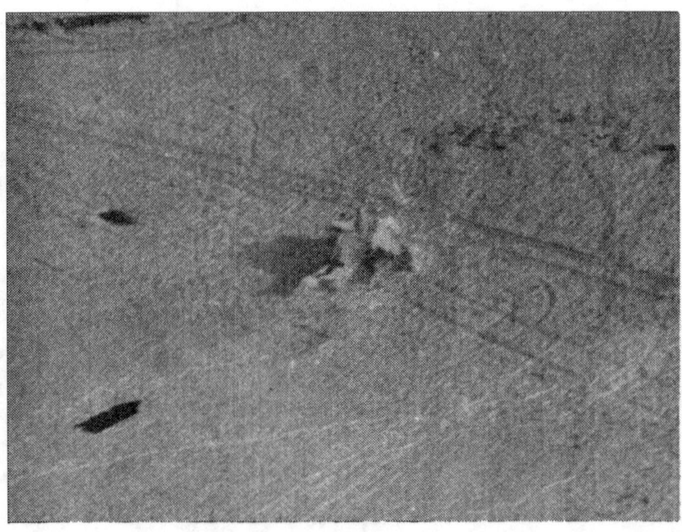

Plate 170

Hay

187. Hay and straw, of all types, are often the lazy man's idea of camouflage.

Plate 171

A little intelligent use of the net, with hay as garnish, might have concealed this truck as a haystack, but the shadow contained by the open back and trapped beneath the vehicle give it away; although the site is appropriate for a haystack.

Plate 172

An untidy heap of hay of this size is unreal even in a farmyard. This vehicle would find better concealment by disguise as an annex among the firm shapes and shadows of the buildings.

Farm structures and debris

Plate 173

188. *Small vehicles.* Sited and concealed with reeds against a reed hut, this vehicle's disguise is further improved by the casual stacking of the timber as garnish against it.

Plate 174

Good choice of site, good positioning. Correct concealment of vehicle characteristics blend this vehicle with the farmyard hut by which it rests.

In both examples the bulk of the vehicle is well related to the site chosen.

189. *Larger vehicles.* A 3-ton truck disguised as a dilapidated building by use of local debris. The vehicle netted between the trees is also well sited.

Plate 175 (War—Germany)

Care is required to avoid too drastic alterations of the appearance of the site.

Plate 176 (War—Germany)

Adapted to appear as extensions to a building. The value of even partial inclusion of the vehicle shape within the original building plan is apparent.

The chassis is very well disguised and the netting extension to the building is firm in shape to match the type of cover.

Positioning the vehicles at right angles against the brick walls is important as this tallies with normal building design.

Concealment discipline

190. Concealment demands discipline.

Plate 177 (Training—England)

Here, human activities in the open nullify the effective concealment of the vehicles.

Plate 178 (Training—England)

191. Keep the unconcealed away from the concealed.

To permit the unconcealed vehicle to park on the sunlit side of the hedge, even for few minutes, is wrong.

Park it either well away from the concealed or within the shade until full netting and garnish is rigged.

Then move to the concealment site and cover and camouflage as quickly as possible.

The other vehicles' concealment fails where their angular shapes show through their nets.

SECTION 27—COLLECTIVE CONCEALMENT

Plate 179 (Training—BAOR—Germany)

192. Three 3-ton trucks netted together and garnished to resemble a clump of scrub (left centre). If this clump had been linked a little more closely to the thicker clumps around it in natural extension of growth it would have remained undetected.

Plate 180 (War—Libya)

193. A group of operational office trucks in an Army HQ camp situated in the white sand dunes around Tobruk. Photograph taken before camouflage. The structure to carry mounded cover is under preparation.

Plate 181 (War—Libya)

The same group. Note the gentle mounding to conform with shapes of sand dunes.

Cover is of undyed white open mesh cloth.

This wartime expedient has now developed into the RASCHEL netting for use in such surroundings.

SECTION 28—Convoys

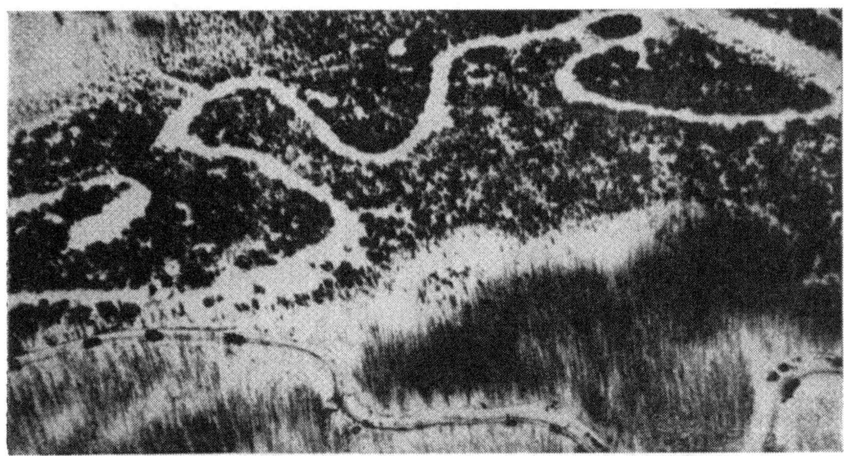

Plate 182 (Training—Canada) An MT column halted

194. The evenly spaced vehicles on the left foreground draw attention in this natural ground pattern, whereas the vehicles on the right cause uncertainty as to which are vehicles and which are bushes, because their irregularity tallies with the natural features of the scene.

195. To halt a convoy like this even for a short time is both obvious and dangerous. Apart from the risk of direct attack, this convoy acts as a pointer to the general trend of transport; which may in turn reveal the direction of a formation's move.

Plate 183 Short halt

What can be done to improve concealment?

(a) The leading vehicles either go under the tree shadow or against the higher hedgerow beyond it.

(b) The middle vehicles go on to the grass verge by the ploughed field on the right as close to the hedge as the ditch allows; thus casting their shadows into the bush shadows instead of on hard bright road.

(c) The rear vehicles. Go into the shade of the high hedge by the verge in the left foreground. A few could also hide among the building and garden pattern on the right. If the halt is prolonged, rig the nets.

This brief plan greatly reduces risks of discovery and attack without hampering movement. Such quick plans require frequent practice during training.

Plate 184 The shadow discloses

196. These vehicles might be mistaken for bushes along the low hedgerow. Their shadows on the road surface are unmistakeable.

Had they sited themselves along the other side of the road their shadows would be broken up among the textures of the ground.

CHAPTER 8—CONCEALMENT OF ARMOURED FIGHTING VEHICLES

SECTION 29—General

197. The modern AFV is large. Many forms of cover that would have hidden a tank in the past are now inadequate.

198. Keep your eye trained to appreciate the size and type of cover that will help you to reduce the bulk of your tank or armoured car.

Plate 185

199. This tank makes good use of the high banked roadside to provide cover from the fire of the enemy.

His position would also aid concealment by reducing the apparent size of the tank.

Plate 186

(Training—BAOR)

200. Remember the AFV's distinctive shape. It attracts attention among other vehicles. These qualities are noticeable in these AFVs moving along a highway in Germany.

Avoid isolated cover

201. Avoid making tracks leading direct to cover especially on soft surfaces. Haystacks are always suspect.

Plate 187 (Training—Germany)

An obvious target for the Air Force to attack.

Plate 188 (Training—BAOR)

202. In contrast with the last picture, here the tank commander understands an AFV's requirements for concealment.

The tank by the silver birch tree has left no tracks in backing off the road into ambush.

The bushes screen the suspension and only the turret protrudes. Even that is sheltered by the tree. The shadow is absorbed against the surrounding bushes.

Damage to foliage

203. Skilful driving and a well trained crew aid concealment. Wanton damage is dangerous.

Plate 189 (Training—BAOR—Germany)

There is plenty of good cover into which these two vehicles could be concealed. Bad crew drill has made the tank position obvious.

Foliage at unnatural angles to normal growth, and allowed to wilt, will give the position away.

Dust and fumes

Plate 190 (War—Normandy)

204. The soft cloud of dust which these AFVs are throwing up may not appear important, but it can indicate their movement along this road to observers a long way off.

Remember dust rises above the cover. This also applies to smoke from exhausts.

Wider spacing between the AFVs and slower speeds are necessary when the route is over a dusty surface and has to be traversed by day.

Study the surface you cross

205. The dust and mud of battle that discolours the hull of the tank brings it in tone with the landscape. This colour is the basic tone of the ground and helps also to conceal the hard shine from the armour. Watch out for any changes of surface soil. A dusty white looks odd against red soil.

Plate 191 (War—Italy)

These tanks moving into action are only slightly garnished with foliage. But they have acquired the soil tone through dust so well that they already merge with the ground, even at this close range. They would be hard to spot from a distance.

Silhouette

Plate 192 (War—Italy)

206. Remember your silhouette. The best cover is useless, and camouflage futile, if your shape looms through it.

Shadow

Plate 193

207. When the sun is bright AFVs cast very distinctive shadows.

Contrast—by shadow and by shine
208. This contrast alone may mark you out:—

Plate 194

The tank out in the bright sunlight merges with the ground in colour and in **tone.** But its dark shadows pick out every detail to make it recognizable.

Steel, even when painted, always tends to shine. The tank in the trees is **defined** by its shine alone.

Avoid both contrasts by keeping well in the shade.

Among buildings

Plate 195 (War—Italy)

209. This tank by blocking the roadway makes itself obvious both to the ground and the air.

There is good shade cover in which to hide.

Tank shapes blend well against buildings.

Plate 196 (War—Italy)

210. Backed into this building this German tank was easy to disguise. A ladder and debris aid the concealment.

Associated equipments

211. The presence of units and specialized equipment that exist to assist armoured formations may disclose the locations of concealed AFVs.

Plate 197 (Training—England)

Wheeled vehicles of an armoured formation, resting in the open with little regard for concealment.

A, B, C, D and E show stores and other wheeled vehicles used for maintenance purposes sited in open with no attempt at concealment.

F a Scammel which indicates possible armoured activity.

212. Tank transporters are specialized vehicles which are not very numerous. Consequently their appearance in an area indicates armoured activities.

Plate 198

Anxiety to hide has only drawn attention. The elaborate foliage may assist at halts but on the road it fails.

The cab of the vehicle and the cupola of the tank project to provide full identification of type.

Concealment in depth

213. The height of armoured vehicles and the shine they produce necessitates plenty of depth in concealment.

Plate 199 (War—Italy)

These well draped nets may look out of place in this Italian olive grove at close quarters, but they provided effective concealment from the air for nine AFVs.

SECTION 30—Track discipline

214. Tank tracks are distinctive and difficult to hide. Every effort must be made to follow the ground pattern. Comparison of tracks enables identification of types to be made.

Plate 200

In this plate note the difference in the appearance of tracks according to the angle of light and softness of texture.

Plate 201

215. An attempt has been made to conform to the ground pattern.

The two tanks are well sited for concealment with good lines of approach, but their location is given away by the tracks on the plough.

These would not have been so noticeable if they had kept to the edge.

Plate 202 (Training—BAOR)

216. An example of bad track discipline giving away the location of AFVs concealed in the wood.

Plate 203 (Training—BAOR)

217. Do not halt at corners or obvious landmarks. When possible always back into concealment. Intelligent use of the available cover would have made these tanks less obvious.

Plate 204 (Training—BAOR)

218. Another example of bad track discipline.

If this AFV had been guided directly into position along the shelter of the wood, it would not have given itself away by the track marks it has made in the field.

SECTION 31—**Prepared positions**

219. When tactically sited the mechanical or hand dug position gives surprise and protection.

220. Where suitable hollows already exist a bulldozer can provide quickly an adequate depth of cover; but the spoil and all tracks created by this work must be concealed.

Plate 205 A prepared pit

221. In this bulldozed pit the foreground has been re-turfed and all the excess spoil distributed into the shade of the copse behind and there concealed beneath fallen leaves. The AFV can vacate the pit either forward or in reverse. The NCO indicates the depth of the pit into which the tank would be netted for concealment.

222. The same bulldozed pit after occupation.

Plate 206

From this position the AFV could engage targets.

The surrounding vegetation has been preserved as much as possible to give natural cover. The netting and garnishing does not blind the tank. Particular care is taken to disguise the long gun barrel and hessian sheet prevents any shine from the turret plating.

All track markings of approach to the site have been either turfed over or removed.

Shallow digging by hand

223. It is not always possible to carry out the major excavations which are required to dig a tank in completely.

Plate 207

The water level at this site is only 2 feet below the ground surface. Nevertheless this depth plus the banking of the spoil will provide sufficient cover to disguise the AFVs' suspension and allow the bulk of the vehicle to be netted into an inconspicuous mound. Note the undisturbed saplings on either side that will add realism to the garnish. This pit should be kept camouflaged when vacant as well as when occupied by the AFV. The site must also be camouflaged while under preparation.

The roadside site allows the AFV to back in position without leaving any track marks of approach.

All spoil is covered and returfed at the entrance and on the mounds.

CHAPTER 9—THE CONCEALMENT OF ARTILLERY

SECTION 32—General

224. The concealment of artillery does not concern the single gun alone, but includes the concealment of the troop, battery and regiment with its attendant vehicles.

Deployment of artillery

225. In deploying a troop, battery or regiment the main concealment problems are:—

  (*a*) How to conceal the lay-out of several guns and gun pits which must be sited near to each other for reasons of command and control.

  (*b*) How to aid the concealment of each individual gun, not forgetting initial tracks to the gun position.

  (*c*) How to avoid too obvious tracks between the gun positions and the wagon lines.

Plate 208 (Training—BAOR)

A battery position in course of preparation with a disregard for all concealment precautions.

Tie in with the ground pattern

Plate 209 (Training —BAOR)

226. The troop has made good use of the hedge and road line in which to site its guns on either side of the roadway.

On the left behind the guns the normal farm and track pattern allows the lines of communication and supply to follow these existing trends and tracks to the gun area.

Plate 210 (Training—BAOR)

227. This troop is well sited along the edge of the track. This allows communication to the guns without causing fresh track markings. Good use is made of the growing foliage to assist concealment. No matter how well a position is concealed it will almost certainly be disclosed by military litter left in the open. In this example no attempt is made to conceal a tarpaulin covering ammunition beside the gun.

228. Lessons learned on too familiar training grounds may be misapplied unless adaptability to other conditions is encouraged.

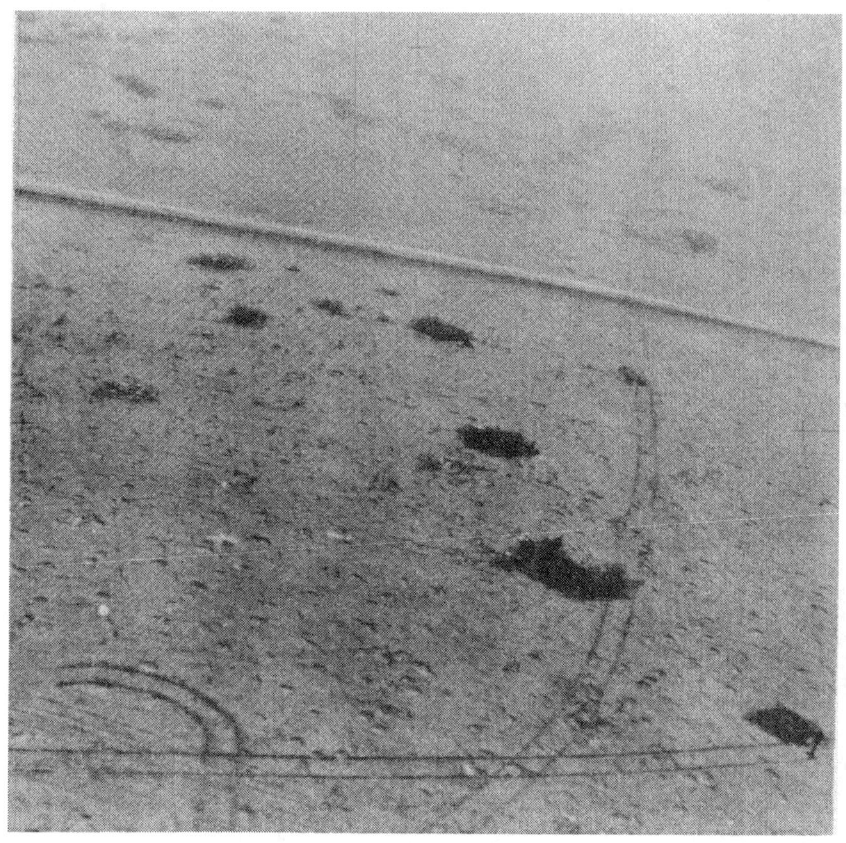

Plate 211 (Training—Larkhill)

The lay-out of this troop of 25 prs has been sited to fit in with the ground pattern. Tracks by-pass the concealed gun positions. It is difficult to tell which are guns and vehicles and which are natural gorse bushes.

Plate 212

229. A troop of 25 prs sited in a regular lay-out of guns and gun-towing vehicles on open farmland.

There is no attempt to conform with the ground pattern and the netted guns produce unusual looking shapes foreign to this area.

The guns here would have been better sited in the wooded areas close by.

Points that disclose your position

Plate 213 (Training—BAOR)

230.
(a) Left: one badly concealed bivouac tent.
(b) Right: one track turn through a root crop.
(c) Right foreground: men in the field by the roadside.
These points catch the observer's eye.
A search within the area then discloses the well sited, well netted 5·5-in gun.

Check your concealment

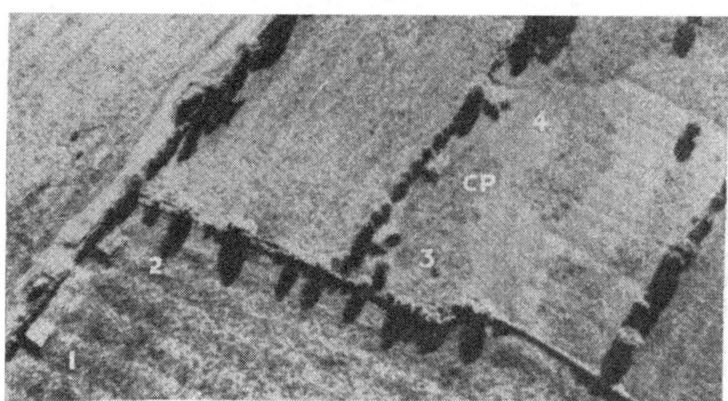

Plate 214

231. When your gun position is complete, ask the air OP to fly over if possible to check faults in your concealment.

A troop of 25 prs well sited within the ground pattern.

The figures indicate the gun positions and command post. No. 1 gun position is made obvious by the self-contained shadow cast by the flat top.

The observation post

232. For observed fire to be effective, observation must be uninterrupted.

The best viewpoint is often also the most obvious choice as a site for an artillery OP and therefore the enemy's fire. This mistake has frequently been the weakness of fixed defences.

Plate 215 (War—Korea)—Hill 187

This strongly built OP gave excellent observation over the enemy position 2,500 yards away.

It was the pride of its constructors; until they found it was always attracting fire.

A more indefinite position on the hillside would have attracted less attention.

The gun pit

233. The gun pit has a distinctive shape. Therefore the first measure is to conceal the site on which the pit will be dug.

Plate 216 (Training—England)

This well hung net has allowed plenty of room for digging. The new sandbags of the revetment show through the net. These then should be toned down as soon as possible.

Plate 217

234. An example of a gun pit nearing completion. The gun shield will need to be toned down as at present it shines through the net.

Plate 218 (Training—England) The gun pit—task completed

235. Dyed hessian used to cover the light coloured sub-soil and sandbag revetments.

Improper use of the net

Plate 219 (Training—England)

236. This gun is not concealed. By stretching the net along the barrel it may provide concealment for the bivouac but the shine from the barrel will attract attention.

This is a common fault. Keep the net propped clear of the gun.

Plate 220 (War—Normandy)

237. Wherever possible the net should tie-in with surrounding cover.

When not in action the gun should be depressed. Nets should not be supported on gun shield but be propped clear.

Artillery concealment sets

238. Concealment equipment used on artillery must give sufficient clearance to allow the piece to be served, and in some cases laid, under cover.

Tubular steel frame supporting the standard type of camouflage nets and providing facilities for partially or completely uncovering the gun for action are being produced.

Plate 221

Plate 222

Plate 221 and 222 show the " CLEGG UMBRELLA " concealment set developed for the 25 pr gun. The set consists of a light tubular steel framework carrying the camouflage net clear of the gun. The centre support for this set is fixed to the gun. This allows for manoeuvrability.

Use of farm vehicles and debris

Plate 223 (War—Germany)

239. A 5·5 gun well hidden among farm vehicles but impractical as clearly the gun cannot be fought from under this heap and its presence will be disclosed as soon as it is required to fire.

Plate 224 (War—Germany)

A 5·5 gun sited and netted among farm vehicles in a farmyard. The varied outlines of farm equipment are useful aids to hiding in this setting.

The 280—mm atomic cannon

Plate 225 (Training—Germany)

240. This is a good example of the use of natural foliage to conceal a very large gun, the 280-mm atomic cannon. Although the track appears to narrow unnaturally it is unlikely a fast moving reconnaissance pilot would spot this unless he already knew the location of the gun. This was confirmed by the pilot who took this photograph. Concealment could have been greatly improved by getting the gun further off the track or, if this was not possible, by placing more brushwood on it in front and behind the gun, so that the track appeared to narrow less abruptly and over a longer distance.

SECTION 33—The self-propelled gun

241. Concealment of self-propelled guns presents similar problems to those involved in concealing armoured vehicles and field artillery.

Plate 226

In this illustration the signature of a troop of self-propelled guns stands out clearly though the guns themselves have left. The irregular pattern and lack of attempt to conceal indicates that they came into action in a hurry and that speed in providing fire support was the most important factor.

These fresh tracks, however, clearly show the type of unit and will lead an air observer to make a close search of the whole area.

Siting

242. There is also danger in similarities of siting and cover.

Plate 227 (Training—BAOR—Germany)

The two SP guns well netted and sited at opposite corners of the same field in the foreground, only caught the pilot's eye through the odd similarity of the two shapes within the one field. Better use of existing cover for one of these guns would have obviated this error.

Plate 228

243. Here, use could have been made of concealment within the ground pattern.

These guns could have been better sited along the scrub on the left of the illustration and one gun at least under the trees on the right. No attempt has been made to conform to a track plan.

Use of camouflage net

Plate 229

244. The SP gun stands over 8 feet in height. Keep it off the skyline and site it in cover that will absorb the shadow and lessen the height from the ground level.

The hull body contains dark shadows when seen from above. It is therefore essential that the net is held well above the superstructure to hide this contained shadow. The barrel must also be concealed.

Use of natural cover

Plate 230 (Training—BAOR)

245. Good sites may be found by reversing the vehicle into cover. This reduces track markings and possible blast effect.

Plate 231

The use of foliage and cut branches placed in natural positions renders this SP gun invisible from a short distance.

Plate 232

246. This self-propelled gun has been driven off the track into the scrub and wooded area, where it is concealed from ground view by natural living foliage. The photograph was taken at very short range; from 200 yards and more it was invisible. It is concealed also from air view. An example of simple quick concealment that has achieved its purpose.

SECTION 34—**Anti-aircraft artillery**

Light anti-aircraft

247. Light AA batteries are employed to provide AA protection at vulnerable points.

248. Positions they adopt may disclose not only the AA layout but also vulnerable points they are protecting.

Rapid concealment in active positions is of the greatest importance.

Plate 233

SP Bofors LAA guns are sited and tied into the hedgerow by an intelligent combination of nets and the natural foliage.

Plate 234

249. An example of concealment set over an L70 Bofors AA gun. The advantages of this set are quick assembly and instantaneous opening when the gun goes into action. The gun can be laid on the target while the gun is concealed.

Plate 235

Air view of the prototype concealment set.

Use of bulldozers

Plate 236

250. Care should be employed where the bulldozer does the digging. Spoil and tracks require elimination immediately afterwards and the gun pit must be concealed without delay.

Heavy AA guns

251. The essential freedom of traverse that AA guns require sometimes prohibits any netting over the guns themselves. Strict concealment discipline must govern everything else about the gun position.

Plate 237 (War—N/W Europe)

Here by good siting and careful netting, concealment is successful, though the smoky cooking fire immediately to the left of the gun rather spoils the effect.

Plate 238

Owing to the obvious similarities of HAA guns on their mountings, variety must be sought in siting their emplacements.

Here effective use is made of a darkened sandbag breastwork garnished with evergreen. All signs of occupation must be covered by brushwood, hessian or other dark materials.

The uncovered helmets on the parapet draw attention to this position.

SECTION 35—The air observation post

252. Light aircraft and helicopters can provide the enemy air observer with the clearest pointers to important headquarters and other worthwhile targets.

Plate 239

Plate 240

The flat shiny surfaces of the light aircraft wings and the bright blade of the helicopter rotor present a considerable concealment problem. The camouflage net in conjunction with canvas blade covers will reduce this telltale shine, but the most satisfactory method is to construct hides into which the aircraft can be run.

Plate 241

A light aircraft successfully concealed in a hide

SECTION 36—**Radar**

Plate 242 (Training—Germany)

253. It is not necessary to have the radar vehicle out in the open, provided that the scanner is clear and free from obstruction.

A radar set (FA No. 1) well sited and concealed by combining the net with foliage garnish. The use of polythene woven material draped over the scanner will assist in concealment and will not effect the echo or deflect the signal.

SECTION 37—**Artillery ammunition**

254. The concealment of the large quantity of ammunition required in battle presents yet another problem. These sketches and photographs give some ideas on how to deal with this problem.

A. Ammunition stacks. As scrub or gorse. (Netting reduced to illustrate)

B. In a hedge or bank. Garnish with foliage or grass tufts.

C. In the wall. Unnetted, but garnished with rubble.

Diagram 6

255. *Ammunition dumps.* The reserve ammunition supply also requires conceal-ment. It should be kept away from the gun positions to avoid clutter. Ammuni-tion supplies can be well hidden along hedges, in ditches and in small stacks beneath trees. Ammunition boxes lend themselves to being " built-in " with walls and built-up man-made structures. Where concealed among natural features their shape requires distortion by propping the net away from the out-line with natural garnish.

Plate 243 Along the garden wall: 25 pr ammunition

A good existing path beside this site allows dumping and removal without any track indications.

Plate 244 (War—Germany)—In the cabbage patch

256. 5·5 ammunition has been stacked and covered with tarpaulins and fits in with this man-made background.

CHAPTER 10—THE CONCEALMENT OF HEADQUARTERS, ADMINISTRATIVE AND MAINTENANCE AREAS AND COMMUNICATIONS

SECTION 38—General

257. The selection of a large country mansion as a headquarters is a frequent practice, as such buildings and their grounds offer many useful amenities. However there are dangers in it and concealment problems.

The practice, being well known, is likely to draw enemy observation. Since neither the buildings nor their grounds are planned for heavy concentrations of men, vehicles and military activities, this is the type of signature the enemy observer may well see.

Plate 245 Headquarters in a large mansion

The signs of heavy track wear and numerous new paths have appeared.

Also may be seen:—

  (a) The converging lines of signal cable routes with signs of line maintenance along them.

  (b) The appearance of a defensive lay-out with section posts, tactical wire and slit trenches.

  (c) New temporary buildings and annexes nearby to house administrative units.

258. *Decentralize.* A more even distribution in an area which contains several buildings is far less obvious.

The main essential is a good normal traffic circuit with an adequate system of hard paths already existing.

Plate 246 (Training—BAOR)

Beside this junction of main roads and the by-ways around it a formation's HQ is housed. The even distribution of offices among a variety of buildings, and the presence of a ready made path system, allows this quiet area to retain its normal appearance. The tree clumps allow cover for car parks for visitors and administrative vehicles.

Plate 247 (Training—BAOR)

259. At the time this vertical photograph of a typical German village was taken, over 250 vehicles were concealed within its boundaries. They remained undetected.

As this area contained a good road circuit, together with the additional advantage of a main road by-passing it nearby, it allowed all traffic to be diverted immediately the approach of enemy aircraft was reported.

This absence of any unusual amount of traffic within the area deceived the enemy observation. The area held the HQ of a corps.

Signboards showing route and location

260. Oblique photographs taken by high speed jet aircraft flying at 300 feet will show formation and unit signs with complete clarity. Tactical numbers are readable without any difficulty and without use of a magnifying glass. AXIS route signs can be clearly seen and entrance signs to headquarters easily picked out. Route and location signs must be made and placed with common sense. They should be kept quiet in tone and concealed from the air.

Plate 248

(Training—Germany)

Headquarters

261. To drape a net over a tent, as in the case of this command vehicle, is useless for concealment.

The guy ropes are a problem in concealment in themselves without being used as props for maps to shine upwards.

The more senior the formation the better the concealment example it should set.

Plate 249 (War—France)—A bad example

Plate 250 (Training—England)—A brigade headquarters

262. By good siting beneath the trees this office tent is well hidden under a net that hangs down from the trees to combine in the natural flow of the foliage and shade pattern to the ground.

The white notice board spoils the concealment.

Never use white notices. Dark wood, russet, or green boards are clear enough at close range. Place them where there is little direct sunlight to make them shine.

Plate 251

(War—Burma—Imphal)

A battalion headquarters

263. This HQ was sited in shelters dug into the hillside and well camouflaged to match the slope.

The unobtrusive roadside site allowed inter-communication without new tracks appearing.

SECTION 39—Structural concealment

264. Permanent camouflage works are usually carried out as a special task under RE supervision.

These examples indicate sites and methods that can be improvised for concealment of headquarters, etc, in the field without specialized skill, provided an adequate supply of material is available.

Plate 252 (War—Korea)

265. This exposed dip in a roadway has been screened in a manner to simulate to distant enemy ground observation an unused road surface above the real one

Note the use of a series of vertical hangings overhead for this purpose. Care has to be exercised by traffic within this screening to avoid creating dust that would rise through the disguise.

Plate 253

266. The much worn pathways between concealed offices and administrative centres are best kept concealed beneath full cover.

This can be done either with netting or, as in this case, steel wire wool garnish over a wire and post supporting framework.

Plate 254

267. This appears to be a quiet woodland glade.

The mounded bank in the foreground is really a framework of braced wires with supporting posts, over which a covering of rabbit mesh garnished with steel wire wool has been placed.

Plate 255

By blending the edges carefully with the natural folds of the ground a perfect "tie-in" of the artificial with the real has been accomplished. Any small blemishes are screened by the natural shadow pattern from the surrounding trees.

Plate 256

268. Beneath these mounds a well built headquarters was hidden. There is plenty of space between the structures and the camouflage cover; so the shape of the office huts is of no importance.

SECTION 40—**Administrative and maintenance areas, dumps and supply points**

Cookhouse areas

269. Cookhouse activities often spoil concealment.

The constant coming and going of vehicles down the track has made its mark on the harder road surface by the mud they pick up.

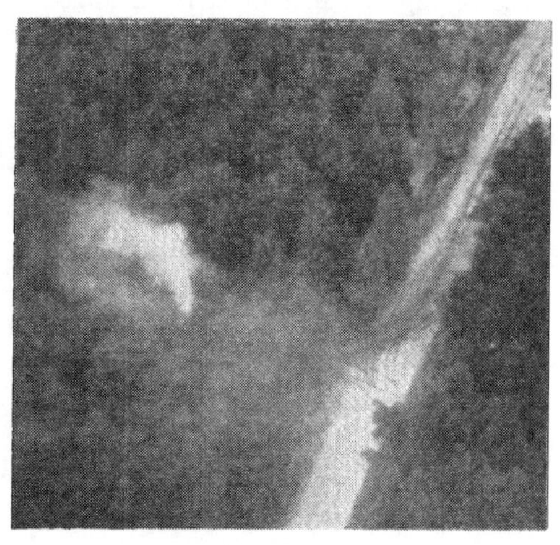

Plate 257

(Training—BAOR)

The smoke from the cookhouse fire reveals the nature of this activity. Use issue cookers and avoid smoke.

Plate 258 (Training—BAOR)

270. Although sited within a wood this cookhouse lay-out shows a correct appreciation of the need for concealment.

271. Well netted over within the shelter of the trees there is a minimum of litter. Everything that would reflect light to the sky is carefully covered from above without hampering the cookhouse functions. The cook truck is well concealed to mask the dark shadow of its open canopy, but the water truck should have its net clear of its shape.

Well organized track discipline around the cooking site is most important as men are apt to take short cuts across the open to speed the delivery of a meal.

The drawing of water for messing needs often produces tracks. Water replenishment should take place by night along existing tracks.

The taking of meals must be arranged under cover as much as possible and the numbers feeding at one time must be limited to avoid crowding.

Concealment of tents and bivouacs

272. The tent pole and ridge lines with the triangular end spaces characterize tents and bivouacs. Try and mask these when you conceal your bivouac.

Plate 259 (Training—BAOR)—Correct and incorrect

Note the indefinite shape of the well netted bivouac in the immediate foreground in comparison with the triangle the pole creates beyond it. The net is held well clear of the bivouac it hides.

273. Tents and bivouacs present flat reflecting surfaces that reveal their positions. This risk is only slightly diminished by colouring the canvas.

Therefore:—

   (a) Wherever possible site your tent beneath cover and in the shade.

   (b) Have a good depth of camouflage above the canvas. Too shallow cover is a frequent cause of the poor concealment of tents. The higher branches of trees growing well above the tent will break up the outlines in addition to the garnish you use lower down.

   (c) Keep the tent flap closed. The black triangle of shadow will disclose as a tent what might otherwise be mistaken for a bush or a mound.

   (d) Maintain strict camouflage discipline around the tent sites. Cover over with leaves and brushwood, or restore by raking over, the track markings and trampling occupation creates on the ground surface.

   (e) Guard against litter.

274. The tracks to the latrines, ablution and messing points made by night can spoil good track discipline by day. Thin guide cords are the best aid for track direction during darkness.

275. The practice of digging-in tents and bivouacs provides good protection and helps concealment. Where this has been done the flattened tent shapes will still require concealment from the air view.

Plate 260 (Malaya—Anti-bandit operations)

276. The Malayan jungle's protecting shadows may not give enough disguise for these tent expanses.

Place some vegetation as garnish to break their outlines in case of observation by enemy ground patrols.

Dumps and supply points

277. By making use of the ground pattern, stores dumps can be laid out with effective concealment. Where stores are stacked around fields and in hedgerows, this is known as perimeter stacking.

Below is an example:—

Plate 261

Stores were stacked parallel with the regular edges of these fields and covered with hessian, earth and grass. An excellent simulation of the irrigation banks was achieved.

Plate 262 (War—Libya)

278. In this case the stacking follows the irregular lines of the Wadi. Rocks and loose stones cover the stores but such ponderous garnish hampers rapid access when the stores are required.

279. Where man-made structures exist either intact or demolished and disused, they are useful for stacking boxes and similar stores against walls, etc, without noticeably increasing their thickness. They can also be used as a false floor to such sites.

Plate 263 (War—Libya—El Alamein)—A dump lining a disused trench.

The character and depth of the trench has not been altered in appearance to the air view.

280. In orchards and plantations small stacks can be placed in the shadow area at the base of trees or among bushes. The stacks should not be too uniform in shape.

Plate 264 (War—Libya)

281. These petrol tins are too regular in their stacking to merge with the natural pattern. In wooded areas there is the danger of over-estimating the cover given by the trees. The tins require coverings to suppress their metallic shine.

282. Where a suitable roadside ditch or hedge exists, it allows an even distribution of stores along its length, without creating fresh track markings. Select the side that is most accessible and, preferably, where the dumps will be within shadow most of the day.

Plate 265

Ribbon stacking

283. Woods provide good replenishment points for supply. But dumped goods and parked vehicles must make full use of the cover away from the roadway itself.

Plate 266

These ammunition dumps may be seen from the air by any pilot following the road from above.

Plate 267 A POL point

284. An idea for the concealment of a roadside POL point. Here jerricans are stacked in six double rows, with camouflage nets thrown over. The nets are garnished with twigs to give the appearance of a hedge.

285. Some suggestions for concealing stores are shown in the diagram below.

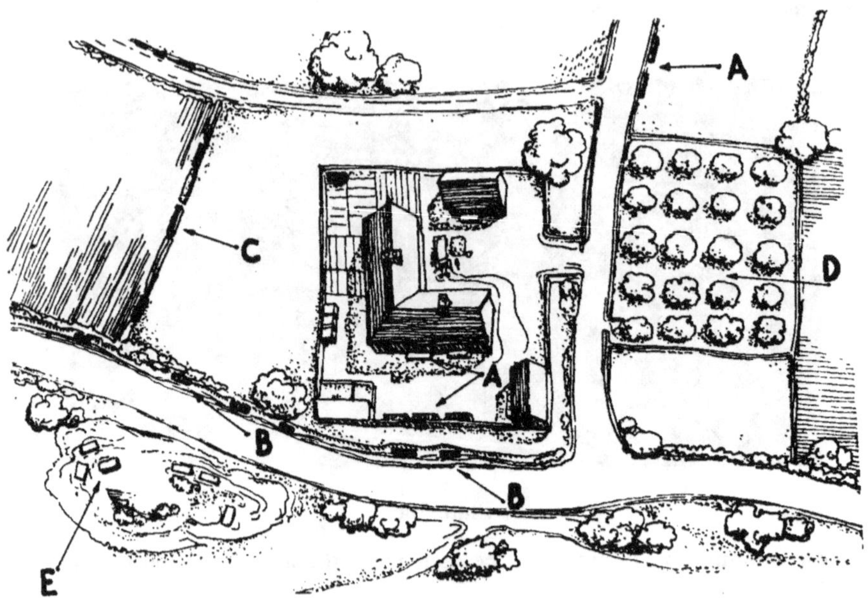

Diagram 7

Suitable sites for stacking

A   Against walls.

B   Along ditches and hedgerows.

C   Filling gaps in walls and hedgerows.

D   Under trees.

E   In gravel pits.

SECTION 41—Concealment of signal communications

286. The distribution and identification of the different types of signal units and equipment is a valuable indication to the enemy of our dispositions and command locations.

287. Signal offices and office trucks are centres of a large amount of DR and similar messenger traffic.

Therefore their locations should be adjacent to, but kept apart from, main headquarters. They should be sited near existing traffic routes to avoid the appearance of many fresh tracks leading towards them.

288. Cable systems

Signal cables, whether overhead, laid on the ground, or buried, are easy to identify from air photographs where they run contrary to the normal ground pattern.

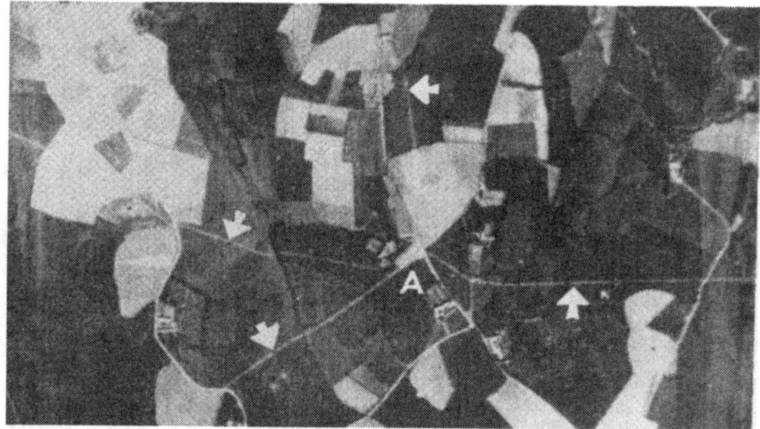

Plate 268 A " Spider's Web " of communications

Concealment around points of origin must be achieved by following the existing boundaries and track patterns closely. Otherwise they will create a local point of communication, as in this picture of a German headquarters.

Wireless vehicles

Plate 269

289. The sign of the wireless vehicle.

The stay wires must be within the camouflage pattern of the vehicles' concealment site. They identify a vehicle whose presence might otherwise be ignored as being of little significance.

Thin wires and slender masts are most apparent against natural backgrounds.

Sites just within woods which provide concealment may have to be accepted in preference to positions giving better wireless reception.

Aerial systems

290. The presence of a tall mast with its attached stays does not preclude all chance of concealment. In this case the clutter of vehicles makes a poor choice of site worse.

Here there is no attempt at concealment.

If the mast was sited at a hedge or road junction, the stronger lines of the ground pattern beneath it may absorb those of the mast and its stay wires.

To site the mast out in an open field is to invite attention.

Plate 270

Mobile radar

Plate 271 A good attempt

291. A mobile GCI station with its radar, operations room, and power supply vehicles.

By simple, yet well thought out, distribution of equipment and vehicles around the tracks and crop junctions this unit has fitted itself so closely into the normal agricultural pattern and lay-out of farming equipment that it is almost unnoticeable.

The concealment and toning down of the movement of scanners is a special problem and is at present the subject of research.

Appendix A

Camouflage equipment—Nets and garnishing

Cat No.	Type and designation	Remarks
	Desert	Natural colour 3 in square mesh net garnished all over with sand coloured knitted material.
	Artillery	
H5/HE 10141	29 ft × 29 ft	} Also for GS use with slit laced.
H5/HE 10131	35 ft × 35 ft	
	GS	
H5/HE 10132	14 ft × 7 ft	
H5/HE 10133	14 ft × 14 ft	
H5/HE 10134	24 ft × 24 ft	
H5/HE 10135	28 ft × 14 ft	
H5/HE 10139	40 ft × 40 ft	
H5/HE 10138	35 ft × 17 ft	
	Light weight desert	Natural colour lightweight net with 8 in square mesh, garnished all over with sand coloured knitted material.
	Artillery	
H5/HE 10309	29 ft × 29 ft	} Also for GS use with slit laced.
H5/HE 10311	35 ft × 35 ft	
	GS	
H5/HE 10305	14 ft × 7 ft	
H5/HE 10306	14 ft × 14 ft	
H5/HE 10307	24 ft × 24 ft	
H5/HE 10308	29 ft × 14 ft	
H5/HE 10310	35 ft × 17 ft	
H5/HE 10312	40 ft × 40 ft	
	Woodland Mk. 2	Nets with 3 in square mesh garnished with green and brown patches; also 2 in strip hessian in green, brown and black.
	Artillery	
H5/HE 10158	29 ft × 14 ft	
H5/HE 10160	29 ft × 29 ft	
H5/HE 10159	35 ft × 17 ft	
H5/HE 10161	35 ft × 35 ft	
	Woodland Mk 3	Nets with 3 in square mesh garnished with 2 in strip hessian in green, brown and black only.
	GS	
H5/HE 10150	14 ft × 7 ft	
10151	14 ft × 14 ft	
10152	24 ft × 24 ft	
10153	29 ft × 14 ft	
10155	35 ft × 17 ft	
10156	35 ft × 35 ft	
	Lightweight woodland Mk 3	Green coloured lightweight net with 3 in square mesh garnished with 2 in PVC strips in green brown and black.
	GS	
H5/HE 10321	14 ft × 7 ft	
HE 10322	14 ft × 14 ft	
HE 10323	24 ft × 24 ft	
HE 10324	29 ft × 14 ft	
HE 10325	35 ft × 17 ft	
HE 10326	35 ft × 35 ft	

Cat No.	Type and designation	Remarks
	Snow	Nets with 3 in square mesh garnished with white calico patches only.
	Artillery	
H5/HE 10174	29 ft × 29 ft	} Also for GS use with slit laced.
H5/HE 10177	35 ft × 35 ft	
	GS	
H5/HE 10170	14 ft × 7 ft	
HE 10171	14 ft × 14 ft	
HE 10172	24 ft × 24 ft	
HE 10173	29 ft × 14 ft	
HE 10176	35 ft × 17 ft	
	Netting Raschel desert	Dyed sand
H5/HE 10290	12 yd pieces 7 ft wide ...	
	Garnishing coloured lightweight	
H5/HE 10104	Black	
HE 10105	Brown	
HE 10106	Green } PVC strip 2 in wide	
HE 10107	Pink } 105 yds long	
HE 10108	Sand	
HE 10109	White	Not for Arctic use.

Miscellaneous camouflage equipment other than nets

Cat No.	Type and designation	Remarks
	Wire netting	2-in hexagonal mesh painted and garnished with steel wool.
H5/HE 10190	Earth } 25 yds × 2 yds in	
H5/HE 10191	Green } in rolls	
	Coir screens	
	Brown	
H5/HE 10201	Large 48 ft × 12 ft	Painted brown on both sides.
H5/HE 10202	Small 24 ft × 6 ft	
	Green	
H5/HE 10203	Large 48 ft × 12 ft	Painted green on both sides.
H5/HE 10204	Small 24 ft × 6 ft	
	Sheets bleached calico	
H5/HE 10211	Large 35 ft × 18 ft	} For use with snow nets.
H6/HE 10210	Small 25 ft × 12 ft	
	Sheets hessian	
H5/HE 10223	Brown 12 ft × 6 ft	
H5/HE 10220	Brown 20 ft × 12 ft	
H5/HE 10221	Green 20 ft × 12 ft	
	Spiders	Steel rod assembly with 6 ribs.
H5/HE 10250	Sets	
	Veils face	
H5/HE 10225	Cotton net 3 ft 6 in. × 3 ft	
	Camouflage cream	
HI/HA 12390	Brown	In 8 oz metal containers.